180 Days

SOCIAL STUDIES

for Second Grade

Author
Terri McNamara, M.Ed.

SHELL EDUCATION

Publishing Credits

Corinne Burton, M.A.Ed., *Publisher*
Conni Medina, M.A.Ed., *Managing Editor*
Emily R. Smith, M.A.Ed., *Content Director*
Veronique Bos, *Creative Director*

Developed and Produced by

Focus Strategic Communications, Inc.

Project Manager: Adrianna Edwards
Editor: Cathy Fraccaro
Designer and Compositor: Ruth Dwight
Proofreader: Francine Geraci
Photo Researcher: Paula Joiner
Art: Deborah Crowle

Image Credits

p.15 Library of Congress [LC-USZ62-83135]; p.17, p.135 (bottom) Chronicle/Alamy; p.19 North Wind Picture Archives; p.35, p.36 NASA; p.37, p.116 Pictorial Press Ltd/Alamy; p.55 Library of Congress [LC-DIG-ppmsca-19305]; p.57 Library of Congress [LC-USW38-000165-D]; p.58 Library of Congress [LC-L9-54-3566-O]; p.76 Library of Congress [LC-DIG-ppmsc-03265]; p.77 Library of Congress [LC-USZ62-60242]; p.90 Dan Holm/Shutterstock; p.91, p.129 (bottom left), p.140 Joseph Sohm/Shutterstock; p.96 Library of Congress [DIG-det-4a20715]; p.97 (left) Library of Congress [LC-USZ62-123757]; p.115 Trinity Mirror/Mirrorpix/Alamy; p.117 (left) FPG/Hulton Archive/Getty Images; p.117 (top center) Ronald Grant Archive/Alamy; p.117 (bottom center) Library of Congress [LC-DIG-hec-13257]; p.117 (right) Library of Congress [LC-DIG-ggbain-25203]; p.118 Library of Congress [LC-DIG-det-4a26409]; p.135 (top) Library of Congress [LC-DIG-det-4a27966]; p.136 Library of Congress [LC-USZ62-6166A]; p.137 (left) Bilwissedition Ltd. & Co. KG/Alamy; p.137 (right) World History Archive/Alamy; p.157 (left), 159 (third down) 360b/Shutterstock; p.158 (center) Goran Bogicevic/Shutterstock; p.158 (second from right) Jeff Gynane/Shutterstock; p.177(top) Library of Congress [LC-DIG-nclc-04337]; p.177 (center) Rorem/Shutterstock; p.177 (bottom) Elbud/Shutterstock; p.180, p.184 (bottom center) Public Affairs Office/The United States Marine Corps; p.182, p.184 (top left) Library of Congress [LC-USZ62-112513]; p.183 Sue Stokes/Shutterstock; p.186 (top) Rob Wilson/Shutterstock; p.188 (center) BravoKiloVideo/Shutterstock; all other images iStock and/or Shutterstock.

Standards

© 2014 Mid-continent Research for Education and Learning (McREL)
© 2010 National Council for the Social Studies (NCSS), The College, Career, and Civic Life (C3) Framework for Social Studies State Standards: Guidance for Enhancing the Rigor of K–12 Civics, Economics, Geography, and History

For information on how this resource meets national and other state standards, see pages 12–14. You may also review this information by visiting our website at www.teachercreatedmaterials.com/administrators/correlations/ and following the on-screen directions.

Shell Education

A division of Teacher Created Materials
5301 Oceanus Drive
Huntington Beach, CA 92649-1030
www.tcmpub.com/shell-education

ISBN 978-1-4258-1394-9
©2018 Shell Educational Publishing, Inc.

The classroom teacher may reproduce copies of materials in this book for classroom use only. The reproduction of any part for an entire school or school system is strictly prohibited. No part of this publication may be transmitted, stored, or recorded in any form without written permission from the publisher.

Table of Contents

Introduction

In the complex global world of the 21st century, it is essential for citizens to have the foundational knowledge and analytic skills to understand the barrage of information surrounding them. An effective social studies program will provide students with these analytic skills and prepare them to understand and make intentional decisions about their country and the world. A well-designed social studies program develops active citizens who are able to consider multiple viewpoints and the possible consequences of various decisions.

The four disciplines of social studies enable students to understand their relationships with other people—those who are similar and those from diverse backgrounds. Students come to appreciate the foundations of the American democratic system and the importance of civic involvement. They have opportunities to understand the historic and economic forces that have resulted in the world and United States of today. They will also explore geography to better understand the nature of Earth and the effects of human interactions.

It is essential that social studies addresses more than basic knowledge. In each grade, content knowledge is a vehicle for students to engage in deep, rich thinking. They must problem solve, make decisions, work cooperatively as well as alone, make connections, and make reasoned value judgments. The world and the United States are rapidly changing. Students must be prepared for the world they will soon lead.

The Need for Practice

To be successful in today's social studies classrooms, students must understand both basic knowledge and the application of ideas to new or novel situations. They must be able to discuss and apply their ideas in coherent and rational ways. Practice is essential if they are to internalize social studies concepts, skills, and big ideas. Practice is crucial to help students have the experience and confidence to apply the critical-thinking skills needed to be active citizens in a global society.

Introduction *(cont.)*

Understanding Assessment

In addition to providing opportunities for frequent practice, teachers must be able to assess students' understanding of social studies concepts, big ideas, vocabulary, and reasoning. This is important so teachers can effectively address students' misconceptions and gaps, build on their current understanding, and challenge their thinking at an appropriate level. Assessment is a long-term process that involves careful analysis of student responses from a multitude of sources. In the social studies context, this could include classroom discussions, projects, presentations, practice sheets, or tests. When analyzing the data, it is important for teachers to reflect on how their teaching practices may have influenced students' responses and to identify those areas where additional instruction may be required. Essentially, the data gathered from assessment should be used to inform instruction: to slow down, to continue as planned, to speed up, or to reteach in a new way.

Best Practices for This Series

- Use the practice pages to introduce important social studies topics to your students.

- Use the Weekly Topics and Themes chart from pages 5–7 to align the content to what you're covering in class. Then, treat the pages in this book as jumping off points for that content.

- Use the practice pages as formative assessment of the key social studies disciplines: history, civics, geography, and economics.

- Use the weekly themes to engage students in content that is new to them.

- Encourage students to independently learn more about the topics introduced in this series.

- Challenge students with some of the more complex weeks by leading teacher-directed discussions of the vocabulary and concepts presented.

- Support students in practicing the varied types of questions asked throughout the practice pages.

- Use the texts in this book to extend your teaching of close reading, responding to text-dependent questions, and providing evidence for answers.

© *Shell Education*

How to Use This Book

180 Days of Social Studies offers teachers and parents a full page of social studies practice for each day of the school year.

Weekly Structure

These activities reinforce grade-level skills across a variety of social studies concepts. The content and questions are provided as full practice pages, making them easy to prepare and implement as part of a classroom routine or for homework.

Every practice page provides content, questions, and/or tasks that are tied to a social studies topic and standard. Students are given opportunities for regular practice in social studies, allowing them to build confidence through these quick standards-based activities.

Weekly Topics and Themes

The activities are organized by a weekly topic within one of the four social studies disciplines: history, civics, geography, and economics. The following chart shows the topics that are covered during each week of instruction:

Week	Discipline	Social Studies Topic	NCSS Theme
1	History	Compare/contrast family/other people of past and today who have shaped the local community	Time, Continuity, and Change
2	Civics	Rights, responsibilities, characteristics of good citizenship	Civic Ideals and Practices
3	Geography	Mapping skills—Simple maps of familiar places: school, community	People, Places, and Environments
4	Economics	Goods and services (local and other communities) and allocation	Production, Distribution, and Consumption
5	History	Historical figures/heroes such as Sally Ride, Marie Curie, etc.	Culture
6	Civics	Symbols of American citizenship	Power, AUthority, and Governance
7	Geography	Mapping skills—Compass rose; read, locate: state, country, state and nation capitals	People, Places, and Environments
8	Economics	Saving vs. spending	Production, Distribution, and Consumption

How to Use This Book *(cont.)*

Week	Discipline	Social Studies Topic	NCSS Theme
9	History	Past historical figures such as Abraham Lincoln, Sitting Bull, George Washington Carver, Jackie Robinson	Individuals, Groups, and Institutions
10	Civics	National and state symbols: birds, flowers, patriotic symbols	Civic Ideals and Practices
11	Geography	Mapping skills—Read, locate: North America and other continents, Canada, Mexico, the equator, oceans	People, Places, and Environments
12	Economics	Market structure—Prices (local and elsewhere), buying, selling, trading; role of producer/consumer	Production, Distribution, and Consumption
13	History	Past historical figures such as Louis Pasteur, Golda Meir, Albert Einstein, Alexander Graham Bell	Time, Continuity, and Change
14	Civics	Justice—Laws and rules in school and the community	Power, Authority, and Governance
15	Geography	Cultural and environmental characteristics of communities	People, Places, and Environments
16	Economics	Government-provided goods and services	Production, Distribution, and Consumption
17	History	Then and now daily life—Clothing, activities, foods, school, houses	Culture
18	Civics	Elected officials of the executive branch	Power, Authority, and Governance
19	Geography	How weather, seasons, and climate affect peoples' lives in a communities and regions	People, Places and Environments
20	Economics	Scarcity and decision making	Production, Distribution, and Consumption
21	History	Lives and contributions of American Indians	People, Places, and Environments
22	Civics	Authority and role of government	Power, Authority, and Governance

© Shell Education

How to Use This Book (cont.)

Week	Discipline	Social Studies Topic	NCSS Theme
23	Geography	Settlement patterns—Where people live and why	People, Places, and Environments
24	Economics	Income earning	Production, Distribution, and Consumption
25	History	Major science and technology inventions/ discoveries—Transportation, and how these changed lives	Time, Continuity, and Change
26	Civics	Basic principles of democracy—Equality, fairness, respect for authority and rules	Civic Ideals and Practices
27	Geography	How people modify the physical environment—Roads, clearing land, etc. and positive/ negative consequences	People, Places, and Environments
28	Economics	Cost of production—Human, natural and capital resources	Production, Distribution, and Consumption
29	History	Major science and technology inventions/ discoveries and their impact	Time, Continuity, and Change
30	Civics	Taxation and community services	Civic Ideals and Practices
31	Geography	Consumption—How people depend on the environment	People, Places, and Environments
32	Economics	Role of banks in the economy	Production, Distribution, and Consumption
33	History	Changes in the local community, over time (roads, buildings, transportation, population)	Time, Continuity, and Change
34	Civics	Historical figures who exemplified good citizenship	Civic Ideals and Practices
35	Geography	Why people/ideas/ things move from one place to another	People, Places, and Environments
36	Economics	Production from natural resource to finished product	Production, Distribution, and Consumption

© Shell Education

How to Use This Book *(cont.)*

Using the Practice Pages

Practice pages provide instruction and assessment opportunities for each day of the school year. Days 1 to 4 provide content in short texts or graphics followed by related questions or tasks. Day 5 provides an application task based on the week's work.

All four social studies disciplines are practiced. There are nine weeks of topics for each discipline. The discipline is indicated on the margin of each page.

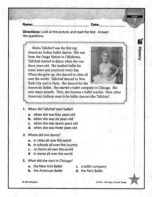

Day 1: Students read a text about the weekly topic and answer questions. This day provides a general introduction to the week's topic.

Day 2: Students read a text and answer questions. Typically, this content is more specialized than Day 1.

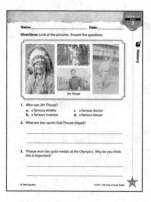

Day 3: Students analyze a primary source or other graphic (chart, table, graph, or infographic) related to the weekly topic and answer questions.

© *Shell Education*

How to Use This Book *(cont.)*

Using the Practice Pages *(cont.)*

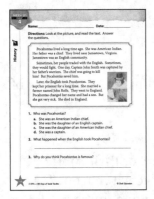

Day 4: Students analyze an image or text and answer questions. Then, students make connections to their own lives.

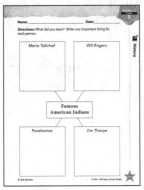

Day 5: Students analyze a primary source or other graphic and respond to it using knowledge they've gained throughout the week. This day serves as an application of what they've learned.

Diagnostic Assessment

Teachers can use the practice pages as diagnostic assessments. The data analysis tools included with the book enable teachers or parents to quickly score students' work and monitor their progress. Teachers and parents can see which skills students may need to target further to develop proficiency.

Students will learn skills to support informational text analysis, primary source analysis, how to make connections to self, and how to apply what they learned. To assess students' learning in these areas, check their answers based on the answer key or use the *Response Rubric* (page 208) for constructed-response questions that you want to evaluate more deeply. Then, record student scores on the *Practice Page Item Analysis* (page 209). You may also wish to complete a *Student Item Analysis by Discipline* for each student (pages 210–211). These charts are also provided in the Digital Resources as PDFs, *Microsoft Word®* files, and *Microsoft Excel®* files. Teachers can input data into the electronic files directly on the computer, or they can print the pages. See page 215 for more information.

Diagnostic Assessment *(cont.)*

Practice Page Item Analyses

Every four weeks, follow these steps:

- Choose the four-week range you're assessing in the first row.

- Write or type the students' names in the far left column. Depending on the number of students, more than one copy of the form may be needed.

    - The skills are indicated across the top of the chart.

- For each student, record how many correct answers they gave and/or their rubric scores in the appropriate columns. There will be four numbers in each cell, one for each week. You can view which students are or are not understanding the social studies concepts or student progress after multiple opportunities to respond to specific text types or question forms.

- Review students' work for the first four sections. Add the scores for each student, and write that sum in the far right column. Use these scores as benchmarks to determine how each student is performing.

Student Item Analyses by Discipline

For each discipline, follow these steps:

- Write or type the student's name on the top of the charts.

    - The skills are indicated across the tops of the charts.

- Select the appropriate discipline and week.

- For each student, record how many correct answers they gave and/or their rubric scores in the appropriate columns. You can view which students are or are not understanding each social studies discipline or student progress after multiple opportunities to respond to specific text types or question forms.

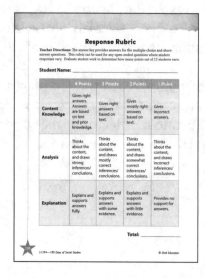

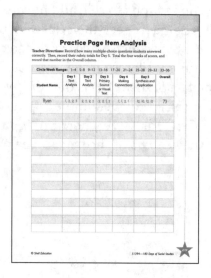

How to Use This Book *(cont.)*

Using the Results to Differentiate Instruction

Once results are gathered and analyzed, teachers can use the results to inform the way they differentiate instruction. The data can help determine which social studies skills and content are the most difficult for students and which students need additional instructional support and continued practice. Depending on how often the practice pages are scored, results can be considered for instructional support on a weekly or monthly basis.

Whole-Class Support

The results of the diagnostic analysis may show that the entire class is struggling with a particular concept or group of concepts. If these concepts have been taught in the past, this indicates that further instruction or reteaching is necessary. If these concepts have not been taught in the past, this data is a great preassessment and demonstrate that students do not have a working knowledge of the concepts. Thus, careful planning for the length of the unit(s) or lesson(s) must be considered, and extra front-loading may be required.

Small-Group or Individual Support

The results of the diagnostic analysis may show that an individual or a small group of students is struggling with a particular concept or group of concepts. If these concepts have been taught in the past, this indicates that further instruction or reteaching is necessary. Consider pulling aside these students while others are working independently to instruct further on the concept(s). You can also use the result to help identify individuals or groups of proficient students who are ready for enrichment or above-grade-level instruction. These students may benefit from independent learning contracts or more challenging activities.

Digital Resources

The Digital Resources contain PDFs and editable digital copies of the rubrics and item analysis pages. See page 215 for more information.

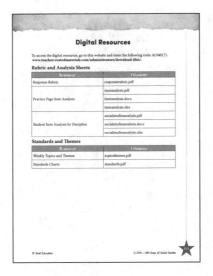

Standards Correlations

Shell Education is committed to producing educational materials that are research and standards based. In this effort, we have correlated all products to the academic standards of all 50 states, the District of Columbia, the Department of Defense Dependent Schools, and the Canadian provinces.

How to Find Standards Correlations

To print a customized correlation report of this product for your state, visit our website at **www.teachercreatedmaterials.com/administrators/correlations/** and follow the online directions. If you require assistance in printing correlation reports, please contact the Customer Service Department at 1-877-777-3450.

Purpose and Intent of Standards

The Every Student Succeeds Act (ESSA) mandates that all states adopt challenging academic standards that help students meet the goal of college and career readiness. While many states already adopted academic standards prior to ESSA, the act continues to hold states accountable for detailed and comprehensive standards.

Standards are designed to focus instruction and guide adoption of curricula. Standards are statements that describe the criteria necessary for students to meet specific academic goals. They define the knowledge, skills, and content students should acquire at each level. Standards are also used to develop standardized tests to evaluate students' academic progress. Teachers are required to demonstrate how their lessons meet state standards. State standards are used in the development of all of our products, so educators can be assured they meet the academic requirements of each state.

NCSS Standards and the C3 Framework

The lessons in this book are aligned to the National Council for the Social Studies (NCSS) standards and the C3 Framework. The chart on pages 5–7 lists the NCSS themes used throughout this book.

McREL Compendium

Each year, McREL analyzes state standards and revises the compendium to produce a general compilation of national standards. The chart on pages 12–14 correlates specific McREL standards to the content covered each week.

© Shell Education

Standards Correlations *(cont.)*

Week	McREL Standard
1	Understands family life now and in the past, and family life in various places long ago.
2	Understands the sources, purposes, and functions of law, and the importance of the rule of law for the protection of individual rights and the common good.
3	Understands the characteristics and uses of maps, globes, and other geographic tools and technologies.
4	Understands basic features of market structures and exchanges.
5	Understands how democratic values came to be, and how they have been exemplified by people, events, and symbols.
6	Understands ideas about civic life, politics, and government.
7	Knows the location of places, geographic features, and patterns of the environment.
8	Understands basic features of market structures and exchanges.
9	Understands how democratic values came to be, and how they have been exemplified by people, events, and symbols.
10	Understands ideas about civic life, politics, and government.
11	Knows the location of places, geographic features, and patterns of the environment.
12	Understands basic features of market structures and exchanges.
13	Understands how democratic values came to be, and how they have been exemplified by people, events, and symbols.
14	Understands the sources, purposes, and functions of law, and the importance of the rule of law for the protection of individual rights and the common good.
15	Understands the physical and human characteristics of place Understands the nature and complexity of Earth's cultural mosaics.
16	Understands the roles government plays in the United States economy.
17	Understands family life now and in the past, and family life in various places long ago.
18	Understands ideas about civic life, politics, and government.
19	Understands the concept of regions Understands the physical and human characteristics of place.
20	Understands that scarcity of productive resources requires choices that generate opportunity costs.
21	Understands the folklore and other cultural contributions from various regions of the United States and how they helped to form a national heritage.
22	Understands ideas about civic life, politics, and government.

Standards Correlations *(cont.)*

Week	McREL Standard
23	Understands the physical and human characteristics of place. Understands the patterns of human settlement and their causes.
24	Understands that scarcity of productive resources requires choices that generate opportunity costs. Understands basic features of market structures and exchanges.
25	Understands the folklore and other cultural contributions from various regions of the United States and how they helped to form a national heritage.
26	Understands ideas about civic life, politics, and government.
27	Understands the physical and human characteristics of place. Understands how human actions modify the physical environment.
28	Understands that scarcity of productive resources requires choices that generate opportunity costs.
29	Understands major discoveries in science and technology, some of their social and economic effects, and the major scientists and inventors responsible for them.
30	Understands how certain character traits enhance citizens' ability to fulfill personal and civic responsibilities. Understands the roles of voluntarism and organized groups in American social and political life.
31	Understands the changes that occur in the meaning, use, distribution and importance of resources. Understands how human actions modify the physical environment.
32	Understands that scarcity of productive resources requires choices that generate opportunity costs.
33	Understands the history of a local community and how communities in North America varied long ago.
34	Understands how certain character traits enhance citizens' ability to fulfill personal and civic responsibilities.
35	Understands the characteristics and uses of spatial organization of Earth's surface. Understands the changes that occur in the meaning, use, distribution and importance of resources.
36	Understands that scarcity of productive resources requires choices that generate opportunity costs.

© Shell Education

Name: _____ **Date:** _____

Directions: Look at the picture, and read the text. Answer the questions.

A long time ago, there were no police in the towns. Some men wanted to help. They joined a watch group. The watch group kept families safe. They lit street lamps. They helped find lost children. They helped find runaway pets. They arrested criminals. They helped in many ways.

The towns got bigger and bigger. The watch groups could not keep everyone safe. So, police forces were created. They kept people in towns and cities safe. Police were important in the community.

1. A long time ago, the towns were smaller. Who kept people safe?
   a. police
   b. watch groups
   c. farmers
   d. coopers

2. More people came. The towns got bigger. Based on the text, who kept people safe?
   a. watch groups
   b. sheriffs
   c. moms
   d. police

Name: _____ **Date:** _____

History

Directions: Look at the picture, and read the text. Answer the questions.

Here is a teacher from long ago. She taught reading, writing, and numbers. The children learned history and geography, too. They had to remember what they learned. There were children from first grade to eighth grade in the same class. Most children finished school in eighth grade. The teacher was important in the community.

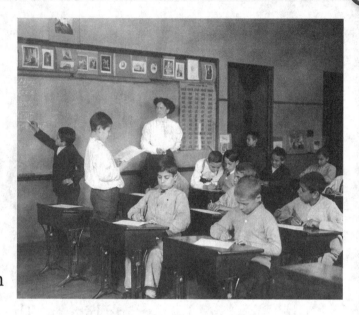

1. What did the children learn in school long ago?

   a. music, art, and writing

   b. art and physical education

   c. reading, writing, and art

   d. reading, writing, and numbers

2. When did most children finish school?

   a. high school

   b. eighth grade

   c. fifth grade

   d. college

3. Why was the teacher important in the community?

   a. The teacher was strict.

   b. The teacher taught art.

   c. The teacher taught music.

   d. The teacher taught children to read and write.

© Shell Education

Name:_____ **Date:**_____

Directions: Look at the picture, and read the text. Answer the questions.

Coopers made barrels that were used to store things, such as meat, eggs, and apples.

1. What did people store in barrels long ago?

  a. wood   **c.** garbage

  b. food   **d.** live animals

2. The cooper would seal the barrels. Why did he do this?

  a. He wanted to make them shiny.   **c.** He wanted the barrels to leak.

  b. He liked to do it.   **d.** So air and water would not get in.

3. Think about the food in your kitchen. What could you store in a barrel if you lived long ago?

_____

_____

Name: _____ **Date:** _____

Directions: Look at the picture, and read the text. Answer the questions.

History

Here are fireworks on the Fourth of July. A long time ago, John Adams said we should have fireworks on Independence Day. This is the day we celebrate that we are free. Light up the sky! The Fourth of July is important to our community!

1. Was the Fourth of July the same or different long ago?

   a. It was the same. Fireworks celebrated that we were free.
   b. It was different. They did not light up the sky.
   c. It was the same. They did not celebrate.
   d. It was different. It was not on the Fourth of July.

2. Why is the Fourth of July important to our community?

   _____

   _____

3. What does the Fourth of July mean to you?

   _____

   _____

51394—180 Days of Social Studies © Shell Education

Name:_____ **Date:**_____

Directions: Look at the picture, and read the text. Answer the question.

In this picture, there is a fire in a town long ago. Everyone helps to put out the fire.

1. Long ago, people helped their neighbors. What do people do to help their neighbors today?

_____

_____

_____

_____

Civics

Name: _____ **Date:** _____

Directions: Read the text, and answer the questions.

> I am an American citizen. I have *rights and freedoms.* They protect me. They let me enjoy my life.
>
> What are rights and freedoms? I am free to do these things. Here are some of my rights and freedoms:
>
> - I can follow my own religion.
> - I can talk about my ideas.
> - I can write my ideas and share them.
> - I can meet with other people.
> - I have the right to be treated fairly and equally.
> - I have the right to a good education.

1. What are rights and freedoms?

   a. things you don't talk about   **c.** things you can't enjoy
   b. things you are free to do   **d.** things you don't protect

2. Which one is *not* true?

   a. I can follow my own religion.
   b. I have the right to be treated fairly and equally.
   c. I can hurt someone else.
   d. I have the right to a good education.

3. Why do we have rights and freedoms?

   a. to stop us   **c.** to silence us
   b. to hurt us   **d.** to protect us

51394—180 Days of Social Studies
© Shell Education

Name:_____ **Date:**_____

Directions: Read the text, and answer the questions.

> I have *responsibilities*. These are things I need to do. I am learning to do them all on my own. I need to do good deeds.

Personal Responsibilities I Do for My Family and Me	Civic Responsibilities I Do for My Community and Country
I am responsible for my actions.	I obey the law.
I take good care of myself.	I respect other people and their rights.
I help my family.	I help my community.
I work hard at school.	I work with others to solve problems.

1. You want to be responsible to your family and yourself. What can you do?

    a. have a tantrum to get what you want
    b. leave your dirty clothes on the floor
    c. do your dishes after a meal
    d. leave your toys all over your room

2. You want to be responsible to your community. What can you do?

    a. be rude to a police officer
    b. not return your library book
    c. leave a mess in the classroom
    d. pick up trash in the park

3. What are two other ways you can be responsible?

    _____

    _____

Civics

Name:_____ **Date:**_____

Directions: Look at the picture, and read the text. Answer the questions.

A good citizen

- helps other people
- is kind
- tells the truth
- respects rights and property

1. Which one is true? I can be a good citizen by _____.

   a. not letting someone play a game
   b. helping other people
   c. telling a lie to get what I want
   d. calling someone a bad name

2. Which one is *not* true? A good citizen _____.

   a. recycles paper and bottles
   b. is kind to people and animals
   c. pushes to the front of the line
   d. tells the truth

3. How is the girl in the picture being a good citizen?

   _____

   _____

Name:_____ Date:_____

Directions: Look at the picture, and read the text. Answer the questions.

Civics

How can we work together? We can work with our family. We can work together with people at our school. We can work with our community. We can even work with people who live far away.

We help people in many ways. We help by getting along. We help by following rules. We can give food and clothing to people who are homeless.

We can protect our environment. We can reuse and recycle. We do more when we work together.

1. Which one is *not* true?
   a. We can work together by following rules.
   b. We can work together by getting along.
   c. We can work together by giving food.
   d. We can work together by starting a fight.

2. What can we do to help people we don't know?
   a. Send money.
   b. Send food.
   c. Send clothing.
   d. all of the above

3. What are two ways you can work together at your school?

   _____

   _____

Civics

Name:_____ **Date:**_____

Directions: Make up a list of four rules for being a good citizen. Think about our rights and freedoms. Think about our responsibilities. Think about ways to work together.

How to Be a Good Citizen
Rule #1
Rule #2
Rule #3
Rule #4

© *Shell Education*

Name: _____ **Date:** _____

Directions: Read the text, and look at the map. Answer the questions.

This is a map of a classroom. It shows the cardinal directions: north, south, east, and west. There is a symbol for each item in the classroom.

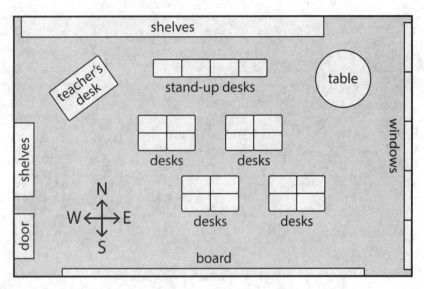

1. What is on the east side of the map?

    a. windows   **c.** a door
    b. shelves   **d.** desks

2. Mark these places on the map.

    • Write A on all of the desks.
    • Write B on all of the shelves.
    • Write C on the table.
    • Write D on the door.

3. Why are there words on the map?

    a. The words make up a story.
    b. The words tell what the shapes are.
    c. There is no reason for the words.
    d. The words make the map look good.

Name: _____ **Date:** _____

Directions: Look at the map of this community. Answer the questions.

Geography

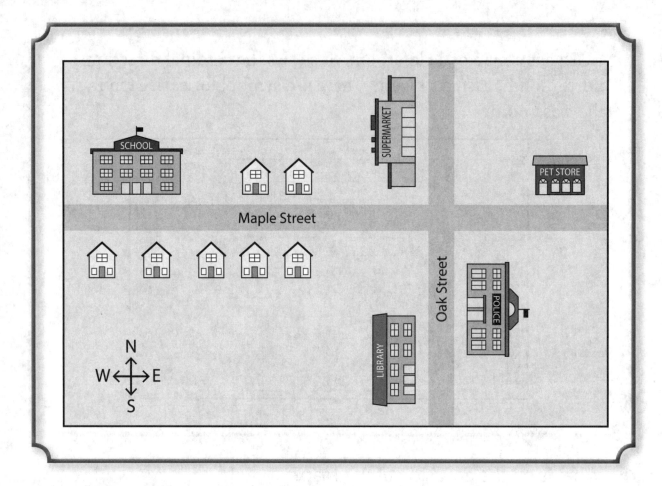

1. On what street is the school?

   a. Oak Street
   b. Maple Street

   c. Library Street
   d. School Street

2. On what street is the library?

   a. Maple Street
   b. School Street

   c. Oak Street
   d. Pet Store Street

3. What two places are on Maple Street?

   a. police station and library
   b. school and supermarket

   c. library and pet store
   d. school and pet store

Name:_____ **Date:**_____

Directions: Look at the map. Answer the questions.

Here is a map of a school community. It has a legend. Look at the legend. It shows what all of the symbols mean.

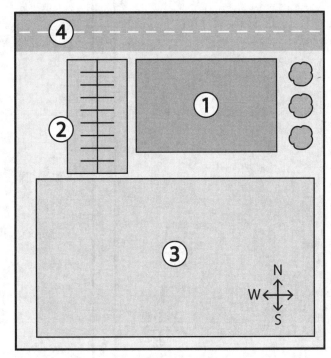
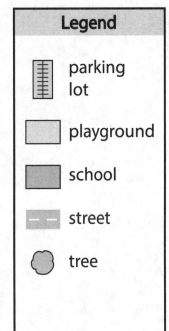

1. What can you find at number 1?

   a. parking lot   **c.** tree
   b. playground   **d.** school

2. What is missing on this map?

   a. street   **c.** East
   b. North   **d.** tree

3. What other symbols could you add to this school community map?

_____

_____

Geography

Name:_____ **Date:**_____

Directions: Draw a map of your classroom.

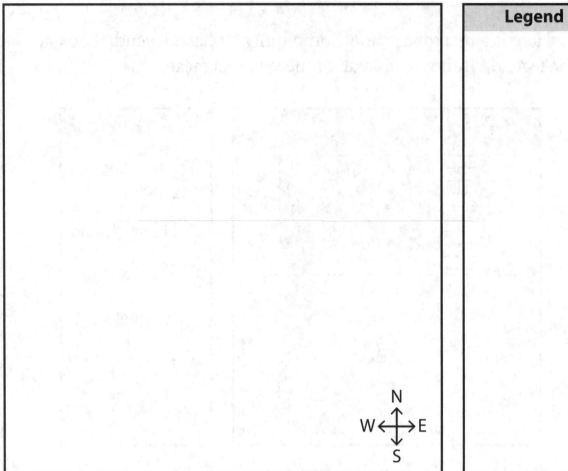

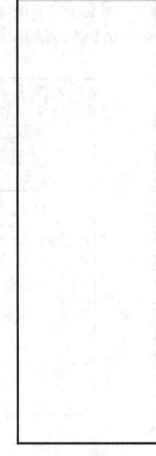

Legend

1. Include at least the following on your legend and map: desks, tables, door, windows, and shelves.

2. Look at your completed map. What else would you like in your classroom? Why?

_____

_____

_____

© *Shell Education*

Name: _____ **Date:** _____

Directions: Look at the map of this community. Answer the question.

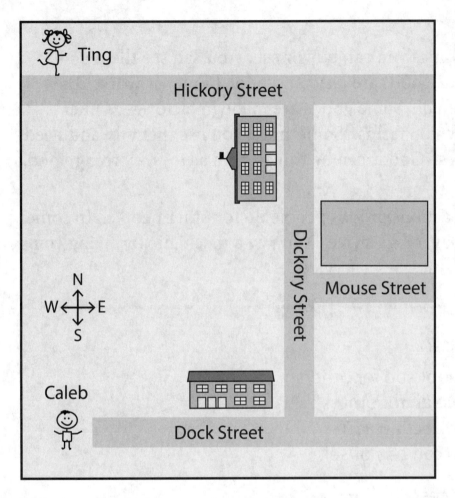

Geography

Ting wants to meet her friend Caleb at the park. Ting goes this way: She walks east on Hickory Street. She turns south. She walks on Dickory Street. She turns east on Mouse Street. She enters the park.

1. Tell how Caleb will get to the park. Use the cardinal directions: north, south, east, and west.

_____

_____

_____

Economics

Name:_____ **Date:**_____

Directions: Read the text, and answer the questions.

Goods are things you can buy or sell. You can see them and feel them. Some goods are used at school, home, or work. They can be big or small. Some goods are made in factories. Other goods are grown on farms. Sometimes, you use them up and need to buy new ones. Goods can be things such as toys, clothing, food, and beds.

Services are actions or jobs people do for other people. In some cases, people pay for a service. You pay a mechanic for fixing your car. The mechanic does a service.

1. What are goods?

   a. actions people do for others
   b. jobs people do for others
   c. ways of protecting you
   d. things you can buy or sell

2. What are services?

   a. things such as food and clothes
   b. actions or jobs people do
   c. food grown on farms
   d. things made in factories

3. Which one is a service?

   a. a toy   **c.** a computer screen
   b. a mechanic's work   **d.** a plate of food

 © Shell Education

Name: _____ **Date:** _____

Directions: Read the text, and answer the questions.

There is a *cost* for goods and services. The cost is how much money we pay for a good or service.

Money is a good. It can be used to buy other goods and services.

We sell a good or service for money. The *price* can depend on how many people want to buy it.

Tyler goes to the store with his mom. He wants to buy a new game. His mom gets it for him because it will be his birthday in a few days. The game is $25. His mom pays the cashier the money.

The good: new game
The cost or price: $25

Economics

1. What is money?

   a. a service   **c.** a good
   b. an industry   **d.** a cashier

2. What was the good Tyler wanted to buy, and how much did it cost?

   a. a game, $10
   b. a toy car, $12
   c. a game, $25
   d. a toy car, $25

3. Which one is *not* true?

   a. There is a cost for goods and services.
   b. The cost is the price we pay.
   c. Money is a service.
   d. We buy goods and services with money.

Economics

Name:_____ Date:_____

Directions: Look at the pictures. Answer the questions.

1. Write **good** or **service** below each picture.

2. You want to have your hair cut. Who do you pay for this service?
   a. a school teacher
   b. a dentist
   c. a farmer
   d. a hairdresser

3. Pretend it's your birthday. What good will you serve your friends?
   a. running shoe
   b. school teacher
   c. pizza
   d. toy bear

© Shell Education

Name:_____ **Date:**_____

Directions: Look at the pictures, and read the text. Answer the questions.

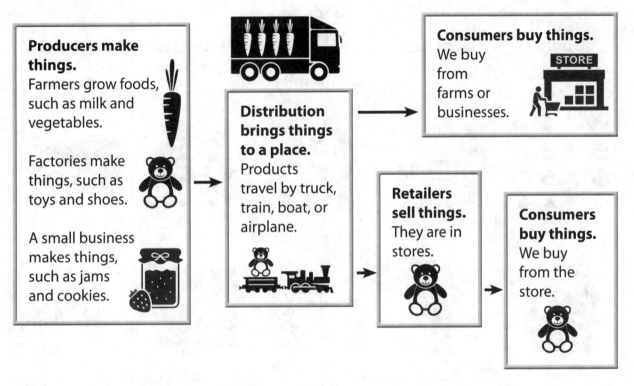

1. Which one is *not* a producer of things your family might buy?

    a. a farmer   **c.** a pilot
    b. a factory   **d.** a small business

2. Think of the food your family buys at the store. How is it distributed to the stores?

    _____

3. Your parents give you a teddy bear for your birthday. Tell the story of how the teddy bear gets from the factory to you.

    _____

    _____

Name:_____ **Date:**_____

Directions: Read the text. Circle the correct pictures in each column.

Economics

Goods?	Services?	Goods and services in your community?	Producers?	Distribution?
 (fruits and vegetables)	 (police officer and car)	 (barber cutting hair)	 (boy and girl)	 (truck)
 (plumber)	 (mail carrier)	 (car on lift)	 (store)	 (train)
 (soccer ball)	 (teddy bear)	 (waiter serving diners)	 (farmer)	 (airplane)
 (laptop)	 (shoe)	 (children playing with blocks)	 (factory)	 (kayak)
 (smartphone)	 (cashier)	 (toy shop)	 (baby crawling)	 (cargo ship)

51394—180 Days of Social Studies

© Shell Education

Name:_____ **Date:**_____

Directions: Look at the picture, and read the text. Answer the questions.

Sally Ride was the first American woman to go into space. She was an astronaut. She worked on the space shuttle *Challenger*. Her job was important. She did research. She worked with satellites. She made a difference. Today, there are many female astronauts.

1. Who was Sally Ride?
   a. a police officer
   b. an astronaut
   c. a librarian
   d. a firefighter

2. Ride had an important job. What did she do?
   a. She flew an airplane.
   b. She worked in a store.
   c. She did research in space.
   d. She worked in a hospital.

3. Ride made a difference. How did she do this?
   a. She was an astronaut.
   b. She worked on *Challenger*.
   c. She was the first American woman in space.
   d. all of the above

History

Name: _____ **Date:** _____

Directions: Look at the picture, and read the text. Answer the questions.

Sally Ride liked science. She wanted all kids to learn about science and technology too. She wrote books about planets and space. She started Sally Ride Science. It helps kids get interested in science. She became a science teacher. She helped children learn about science, Earth, and the planets.

1. What did Ride want all kids to be able to learn about?

   a. science   **c.** physical education
   b. art   **d.** music

2. Based on the text, what did Ride do to help children?

   a. She worked hard.
   b. She learned about space.
   c. She was an astronaut.
   d. She wrote books about planets.

3. How could Ride's work make a difference for you?

   a. You could play an instrument.
   b. You could own a store.
   c. You could learn about science.
   d. You could learn about animals.

51394—180 Days of Social Studies   © Shell Education

Name:_____ **Date:**_____

Directions: Look at the picture, and read the text. Answer the questions.

Marie Curie read a lot and worked hard. She was a scientist. We have better x-ray machines because of her.

1. Why is Curie famous?

   a. We have science because of her.
   b. We have better x-ray machines because of her.
   c. We have teachers because of her.
   d. We have astronauts because of her.

2. How did Curie reach her goal?

   a. She stayed at home.   c. She grew up.
   b. She read one book.   d. She worked hard.

3. What lesson could you learn from Curie?

   _____

   _____

   _____

History

Name:_____ **Date:**_____

Directions: Read the text, and answer the questions.

> Sally Ride and Marie Curie helped many people. So did these people.
>
> | Person | She... |
> |---|---|
> | Harriet Beecher Stowe | wrote a famous book about slavery. |
> | Clara Barton | was a nurse. She started the American Red Cross. |
> | Eleanor Roosevelt | was America's first lady. She worked for people's rights. |
> | Wilma Rudolph | won three Olympic gold medals. She was a teacher and a coach. |
> | Sandra Day O'Connor | was the first female Supreme Court judge. |

1. What is the same about these people?

   a. They were women who were nurses.

   b. They were women who helped people.

   c. They were women who were doctors.

   d. They were women who won Olympic medals.

2. What could you do to be like these women?

   _____

   _____

   _____

51394—180 Days of Social Studies
© Shell Education

Name: _____ **Date:** _____

Directions: Read the text. Answer the questions.

Many famous Americans have helped other people. They made discoveries. They nursed people who were sick. They wrote books. They made a difference.

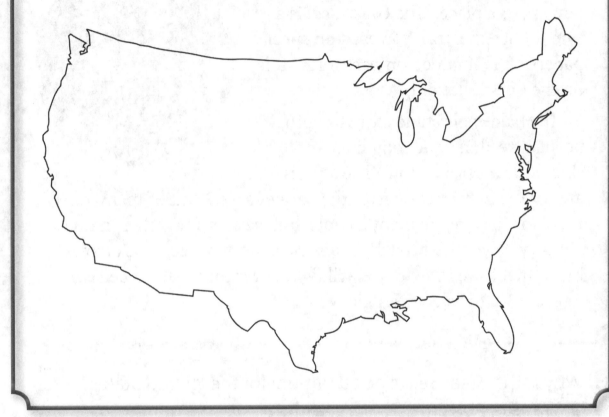

1. Do you know about any famous Americans? They may be athletes. They may be authors. They may be scientists. Write their names on the map.

2. Tell about how they made a difference.

_____

_____

_____

Name:_____   Date:_____

Directions: Look at the picture, and read the text. Answer the questions.

Civics

A symbol is a thing that stands for something else. It may be an object, a person, or a place. The *Great Seal* is a symbol of America. It is used on special papers. It is stamped on passports. It is on the one-dollar bill.

The bald eagle stands for strength, beauty, freedom, and long life. The shield means protection. The stripes are for the first 13 colonies. The banner says, "Out of many, one." It means that we are many people, but we stand together in one country. The olive branch means we choose peace. The arrows mean that if we have to, we will fight a war for what we believe. The stars in the sky mean glory.

1. Why is the Great Seal a good symbol for the United States?

   a. It has a bird and people like birds.
   b. It stands for many important things.
   c. It looks like a nice picture of things.
   d. It's very fancy and nice.

2. Which one is *not* true?

   a. The bald eagle stands for strength.
   b. The seal is on the one-dollar bill.
   c. The stripes are for the first 15 colonies.
   d. The shield means protection.

51394—*180 Days of Social Studies*   © Shell Education

Name: _____   **Date:** _____

Directions: Look at the picture, and read the text. Answer the questions.

The flag of the United States is an important symbol. It is red, white, and blue. The colors have a meaning. Red is for bravery. White is for purity. Blue is for justice.

The 13 stripes are for our first 13 colonies. The 50 stars are for today's 50 states.

1. What do the colors mean on our flag?

    a. Red is for bravery. White is for justice. Blue is for purity.
    b. Red is for bravery. White is for purity. Blue is for justice.
    c. White is for bravery. Blue is for purity. Red is for justice.
    d. Red is for purity. Blue is for justice. White is for bravery.

2. What is the Stars and Stripes?

    a. our Great Seal
    b. the White House
    c. the flag of our country
    d. the Statue of Liberty

3. What does the flag mean to you?

    _____

    _____

    _____

Civics

Name: _____ **Date:** _____

Directions: Look at the infographic. Answer the questions.

She was a gift from France.

The rays on her crown stand for the seven continents.

Her torch lights the way to liberty.

She's on Liberty Island in New York Harbor.

She celebrates freedom for all.

The Statue of Liberty

1. Which one is true?

   a. The Statue of Liberty celebrates patience.
   b. The Statue of Liberty celebrates justice.
   c. The Statue of Liberty celebrates purity.
   d. The Statue of Liberty celebrates freedom.

2. The Statue of Liberty's torch lights the way to _____ .

   a. truth   c. liberty
   b. justice   d. charity

3. What does the Statue of Liberty mean to you?

   _____

   _____

51394—180 Days of Social Studies
© Shell Education

Name:_____ Date:_____

Directions: Look at the picture, and read the text. Answer the questions.

Mount Rushmore is in South Dakota. It shows four presidents carved in stone. They are George Washington, Thomas Jefferson, Theodore Roosevelt, and Abraham Lincoln. Each one did something special for our country. They remind us to be strong and free.

Crazy Horse Memorial is in South Dakota, too. The memorial represents how American Indians changed America.

1. Who are the presidents on Mount Rushmore?
   a. Washington, Bush, Obama, Johnson
   b. Washington, Jefferson, Lincoln, Roosevelt
   c. Washington, Reagan, Carter, Ford
   d. Washington, Kennedy, Truman, Hoover

2. Why is Crazy Horse Memorial important?
   a. It celebrates modern life.
   b. It celebrates railroads.
   c. It celebrates American Indians.
   d. It celebrates enslaved people.

3. How does Mount Rushmore inspire you?

_____

_____

Name: _____ Date: _____

Directions: Write words that come to mind when you see these symbols.

Civics

Our Flag	The Statue of Liberty	The Great Seal

© Shell Education

Name: _____ **Date:** _____

Directions: Read the text, and look at the map. Answer the questions.

Geography

This is a map of a community. You live in a community. A community is a place where people live. They share services. Your home is on a street or road. There are other houses or buildings near your home. There is a school. There may be a library or a church. There may be a park or some stores.

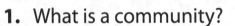

1. What is a community?

   a. It is a place where there are many factories.
   b. It is a place where there are zoo animals.
   c. It is a place where people live and share.
   d. It is a place where boats float.

2. Add the missing cardinal directions to the compass rose.

3. Where are the mountains on the map?

   a. near Green Street
   b. near Red and Green Streets
   c. near Blue and Green Streets
   d. near Blue and Red Streets

Geography

Name: _____ **Date:** _____

Directions: Read the text, and look at the map. Answer the questions.

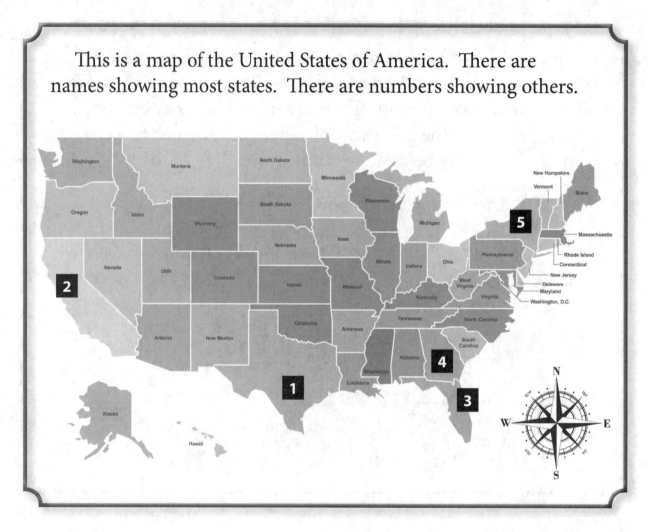

This is a map of the United States of America. There are names showing most states. There are numbers showing others.

1. Find the state of Texas. It is very big. What number is it?

   a. 4   **c.** 3
   b. 1   **d.** 5

2. Find the state of New York. It is in the North and the East. What number is it?

   a. 5   **c.** 4
   b. 1   **d.** 2

3. A compass rose is a symbol. It is used on maps. It shows each of the cardinal directions—north, south, east, and west. Find the compass rose on the map. Color it red.

                    © Shell Education

Name:_____ **Date:**_____

Directions: Read the text, and look at the map. Answer the questions.

North America

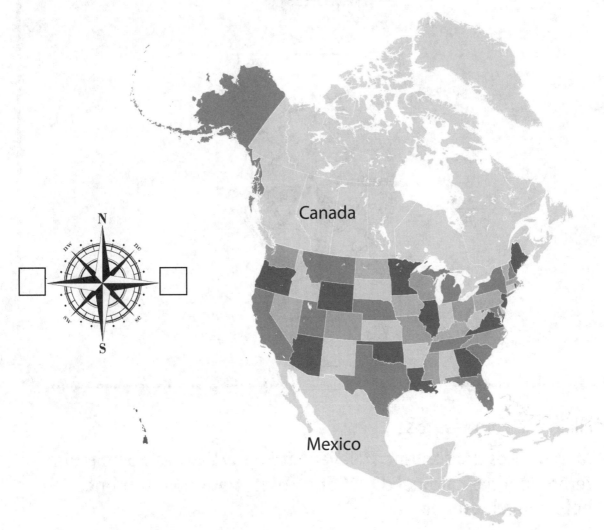

1. What country is north of the United States?

    a. Mexico   **c.** Canada
    b. Central America   **d.** South America

2. What country is south of the United States?

    a. Mexico   **c.** Canada
    b. Central America   **d.** South America

3. Find the compass rose on the map. Add **E** for east.
    Add **W** for west.

Name:_____ **Date:**_____

Directions: Look at the compass rose. Answer the questions.

Geography

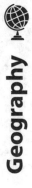

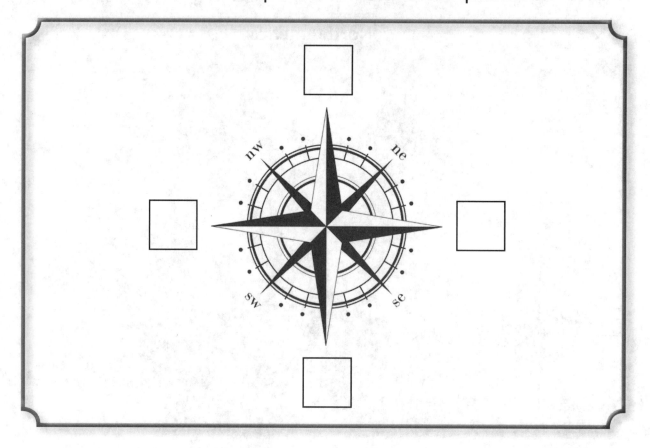

1. Fill in the compass rose.

2. Marcus uses the sentence "Never Eat Soggy Waffles" to help him remember the cardinal directions. Write your own sentence to help you remember.

_____

_____

_____

_____

51394—180 Days of Social Studies
© Shell Education

Name: _____ **Date:** _____

Directions: Look at the map. Read the instructions.

1. Color the 5 biggest states **red.**

2. Color your home state **blue.**

3. Color a state you would like to visit **green.**

4. Draw a star on the place where 4 states touch.

© Shell Education

Economics

Name:_____ Date:_____

Directions: Read the text, and answer the questions.

What are some ways to make money? Mom might make money by working at a job. Dad might be an artist who sells his paintings. Your big brother might babysit to make money. Your friend might sell the bike she no longer rides. You may do chores at home and get an allowance. There are many ways to make money.

What can you do with the money you make? You can spend your money. You can buy something. You can save your money. You might save for a computer. You can donate money. You could give it to a person in need.

1. Based on the text, which one is *not* true?
   a. You can make money by working.
   b. You can make money by doing a service.
   c. You can make money by watching TV.
   d. You can make money by selling something.

2. What can you do with your money?
   a. You can spend your money.
   b. You can buy a service with your money.
   c. You can save your money.
   d. all the above

3. What can a student who is your age buy with money?
   a. a car
   b. a toy
   c. a vacation
   d. a house

Name: _____ **Date:** _____

Directions: Look at the pictures, and read the text. Answer the questions.

Some goods and services are *needs*.

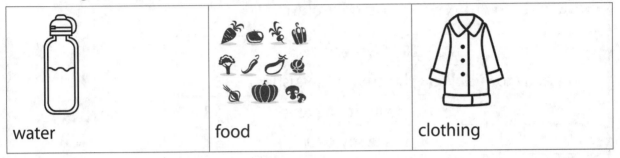

| water | food | clothing |

Some goods and services are *wants*.

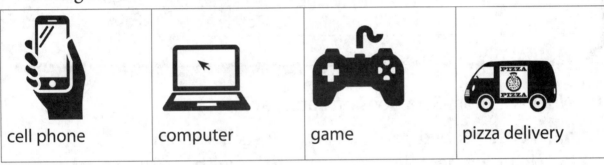

| cell phone | computer | game | pizza delivery |

1. Which one can you live without?

   a. clothing   **c.** food
   b. cell phone   **d.** water

2. Which one is a want?

   a. water   **c.** clothing
   b. food   **d.** game

3. Imagine you have only a little money. Which is best to buy first?

   a. a want   **c.** a need
   b. nothing   **d.** everything

Name: _____ **Date:** _____

Economics

Directions: Look at the chart, and answer the questions.

Sara wants to save money for a pogo stick. She will do chores. She made a plan.

My Chores		
Monday to Friday	help with the dishes	$2
	clean up my toys	$3
	make my bed	$1
Saturday	dust my room	$2
	vacuum my room	$2
	Total	

pogo stick
$30

1. What is a chore Sara does on Saturday?

   a. makes her bed
   b. cleans up her toys

   c. dusts her room
   d. helps with the dishes

2. Sara did all of her chores for the week. How much money did she make?

   a. $5
   b. $10

   c. $8
   d. $7

3. Sara does all of her chores each week. How many weeks will it take to save the money she wants for the pogo stick? Why?

   _____

   _____

   _____

51394—180 Days of Social Studies

© Shell Education

Name: _____ **Date:** _____

Directions: Read the text, and answer the questions.

You get an allowance of $10 each week. Your dad says you must save some money for college. You can spend some money, too. You want to buy treats and go to the movies. You make a budget for your saving and spending.

My Budget		Saving	Spending
Allowance			
Week 1	$10	$5	$5
Week 2	$10	$5	$5
Week 3	$10	$5	$5
Week 4	$10	$5	$5
Week 5	$10	$5	$5

1. How much money will you have saved after 5 weeks?

   a. $10   c. $30
   b. $20   d. $25

2. How much money can you spend on treats and the movies each week?

   _____

3. If you wanted to save more money, how could you change your plan?

   _____

   _____

Economics

Name:_____ **Date:**_____

Directions: Read the text. Answer the question. Make a budget.

How to make money each week:
- Cut the lawn $10
- Make my bed each day $7
- Walk the dog $5
- Other $___

Things I need:
- college (save)
- tablet (save)
- other (save)

Things I want:
- park rides (spend)
- food treats (spend)
- movies (spend)
- small toys (spend)
- other (spend)

1. For each week, choose a way to make money. Think about needs and wants. Choose what to save for and what to spend. Make a budget.

My Budget		
Ways to Make Money	**Saving**	**Spending**
Week 1		
Week 2		
Week 3		
Week 4		
Week 5		

Name: _____ **Date:** _____

Directions: Look at the picture, and read the text. Answer the questions.

History

Abraham Lincoln was the 16th president of the United States. He was a good person. He said all people should be free, not enslaved. Some people did not agree. Slavery caused the Civil War. It lasted four years. Lincoln worked hard to keep the country together. He signed a paper to free the enslaved people. Lincoln was shot on April 14, 1865. The war had just ended.

1. Based on the text, what did Lincoln think about people?

   a. All people should be free.   **c.** People were funny.
   b. Some people were good.   **d.** People should go to war.

2. What did Lincoln do during the Civil War?

   a. left the country   **c.** joined the war
   b. kept the country together   **d.** bought enslaved people

3. How did Lincoln make the biggest difference?

   a. He was shot.
   b. He was a good person.
   c. He freed the enslaved people.
   d. He was a lawyer.

History

Name:_____ **Date:**_____

Directions: Look at the picture, and read the text. Answer the questions.

FIRST: Sitting Bull was a Lakota leader. Many white people came. They wanted to live on Lakota land. He wanted to make peace.

NEXT: The Lakota went to war. They tried to get their land back. But the settlers would not go. Sitting Bull wanted his people to live free on their own land.

THEN: The Lakota and their allies won the Battle of Little Bighorn. But more white people came. Finally, Sitting Bull had to give up. The Lakota moved to a small piece of land called a reservation.

AT THE END: Sitting Bull died in a fight.

1. What did Sitting Bull want to do when white people first came?

   a. make peace   **c.** fight them
   b. hunt   **d.** scare them

2. Why did Sitting Bull and the Lakota go to war?

   a. Settlers wanted Lakota land.
   b. There were no bison left to hunt.
   c. He wanted his people to be free.
   d. Sitting Bull was killed in a fight.

51394—180 Days of Social Studies   © Shell Education

Name: _____ **Date:** _____

Directions: Look at the infographic. Answer the questions.

History

1
There were no schools for black children. Carver had to travel far away to go to school.

2
He became a scientist and a teacher.

George Washington Carver

3
He taught about growing plants, such as peanuts.

4
He invented many uses for peanuts, such as flour, glue, and soap.

---

1. Why did Carver travel far away?

   a. to read   **c.** to see a friend

   b. to go home   **d.** to go to school

2. What did Carver teach?

   a. math   **c.** reading

   b. about plants   **d.** experiments

3. What did Carver invent? How could this help people?

_____

_____

_____

Name:_____ Date:_____

History

Directions: Look at the picture, and read the text. Answer the questions.

This is Jackie Robinson. He hoped to play Major League Baseball. It was a long time ago. Only white players were allowed.

Robinson was very brave. He met many people who were not kind. But he did not give up. He said all people should have rights. Then, in 1947, the Brooklyn Dodgers chose him for their team. He was the first African American to play professional baseball. Now African Americans play all sports.

1. How is Major League Baseball different now for African American players?

   _____

   _____

2. What can you learn from Robinson?

   _____

   _____

   _____

Name: _____ **Date:** _____

Directions: Look at the pictures. Answer the questions.

1. What makes these people the same? What makes them different?

Same	Different

Civics

Name:_____ Date:_____

Directions: Look at the picture, and read the text. Answer the questions.

The bald eagle is a national symbol for our country. The bald eagle is strong. It is loyal. It is a survivor. These are all things we want to be, too.

There is a bird symbol for each state. Here are some of them.

- The bird for California is the valley quail. It is strong. It can adapt.

- The bird for Texas is the northern mockingbird. It is the bird for Arkansas, Florida, Mississippi, and Tennessee, too! It can sing the songs of other birds.

- The bird for New York is the eastern bluebird. It is the bird for Missouri, too. It stands for happiness.

1. Why is the bald eagle a good symbol for our country?

   a. It is big and bright.
   b. It can fly high and far.
   c. It can eat little animals.
   d. It is strong and loyal.

2. Which one is *not* true?

   a. The bald eagle is our national bird.
   b. There is a bird symbol for each state.
   c. The bird for California is the mockingbird.
   d. The bird for New York is the eastern bluebird.

3. What is the bird that is a symbol for five states?

   a. eastern bluebird
   b. northern mockingbird
   c. bald eagle
   d. valley quail

© Shell Education

Name: _____ **Date:** _____

Directions: Look at the picture, and read the text. Answer the questions.

> The rose is the official flower for our country. It stands for love and beauty. This makes it a good symbol.
>
> There is a flower symbol for each state. All of these flowers live in their states.
>
> - The flower for Florida is the orange blossom.
> - The flower for California is the California poppy.
> - The flower for Texas is the bluebonnet.
> - The flower for Vermont is the red clover.
> - The flower for Oklahoma is the Oklahoma rose.
> - The flower for Georgia is the Cherokee rose.

1. What is the official flower for our country?

  a. poppy   **c.** red clover
  b. rose   **d.** bluebonnet

2. What does the rose stand for?

  a. strength and beauty   **c.** perseverance
  b. happiness   **d.** love and beauty

3. Why is the rose a good symbol for our country?

_____

_____

Civics

Name: _____   **Date:** _____

Directions: Look at the picture, and read the text. Answer the questions.

- The Liberty Bell is at Independence Hall in Philadelphia.
- The bell stands for freedom.
- Three bells were made. The first two bells broke.

1. Which one is true?

   a. One bell was made.   **c.** Three bells were made.
   b. Two bells were made.   **d.** Four bells were made.

2. What does the Liberty Bell stand for?

   a. justice   **c.** charity
   b. truth   **d.** freedom

3. Name two other symbols that stand for freedom.

   _____

   _____

51394—180 Days of Social Studies

© Shell Education

Name:_____ **Date:**_____

Directions: Look at the pictures, and read the text. Answer the questions.

The White House is where the president lives. It is a symbol of our country. It stands for freedom.

The Lincoln Memorial has a big statue. It shows President Abraham Lincoln. He freed the enslaved people in our country. The memorial stands for freedom, too.

The Washington Monument was built to honor our first president, George Washington. It stands for respect.

1. How does learning about these buildings help you to be a good citizen?

   a. by learning about how buildings were built long ago
   b. by learning about presidents who were good citizens
   c. by seeing what the buildings look like
   d. by seeing how big the buildings are

2. Which two of these buildings stand for freedom?

   a. the White House and the Washington Monument
   b. the Lincoln Memorial and the Washington Monument
   c. the Lincoln Memorial and the White House
   d. the Lincoln Memorial and Mount Rushmore

3. Which symbol is the most important to you?

Civics

Name:_____ **Date:**_____

Directions: Look at the pictures, and read the text. Answer the questions.

> Symbols stand for key ideas. They remind us of what is important. These are ideas such as *freedom*, *strength*, *loyalty*, *happiness*, *love*, *beauty*, and *respect*.

1. Choose two of these ideas. Tell what they mean to you. How do they make you a better person?

	What this means to me
_____ idea	_____ _____ _____ _____
	What this means to me
_____ idea	_____ _____ _____ _____

© Shell Education

Name:_____ **Date:**_____

Directions: Read the text, and look at the map. Answer the questions.

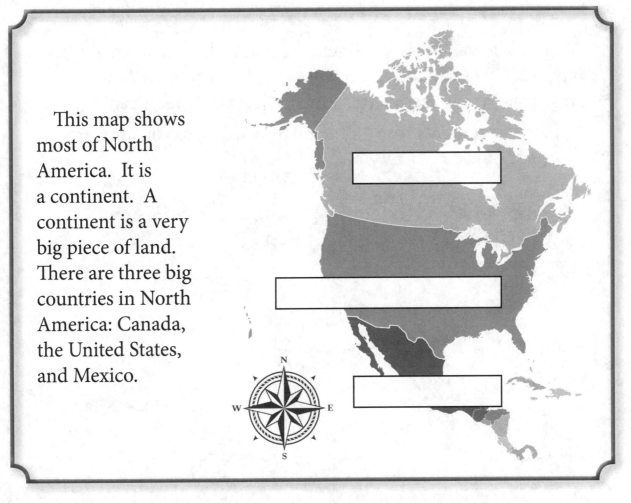

This map shows most of North America. It is a continent. A continent is a very big piece of land. There are three big countries in North America: Canada, the United States, and Mexico.

1. Add the names of the three countries to the map.

2. Look at the compass rose. Where is most of Canada?

   a. south of the United States
   b. north of the United States
   c. east of the United States
   d. west of the United States

3. Look at the compass rose. Where is Mexico?

   a. south of the United States
   b. north of the United States
   c. east of the United States
   d. west of the United States

Geography

Name:_____ **Date:**_____

Directions: Read the text, and look at the map. Answer the questions.

Here is a map of the continents of the world. There are seven big pieces of land. The continents are North America, South America, Europe, Asia, Africa, Australia, and Antarctica.

Find the compass rose on the map. It will help you answer the questions.

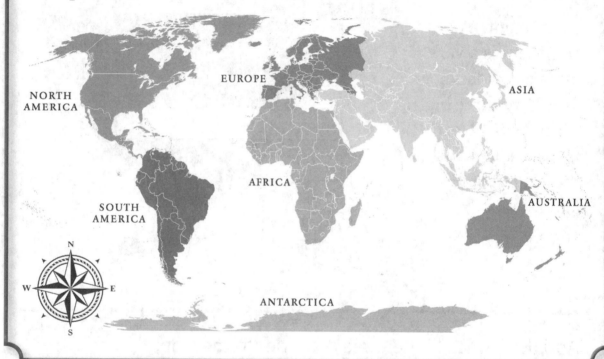

1. Where is the United States?

   a. in South America   **c.** in Europe
   b. in North America   **d.** in Asia

2. What continent is north of Africa?

   a. North America   **c.** Europe
   b. South America   **d.** Asia

3. What continents are south of Asia?

51394—180 Days of Social Studies   © *Shell Education*

Name:_____ **Date:**_____

Directions: Look at the picture, and answer the questions.

This is a globe. It is like a map, but it is 3-dimensional. We need to turn a globe to see all the continents.

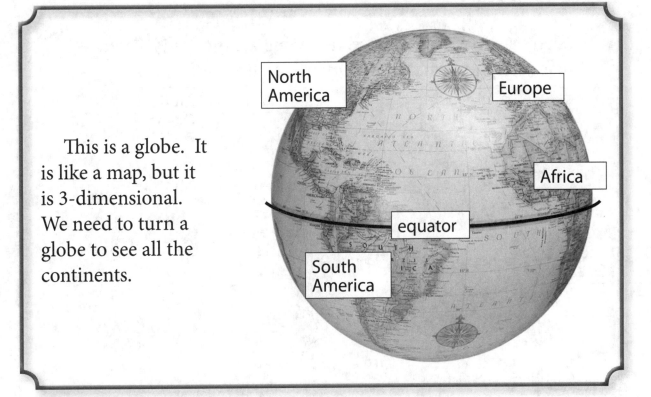

1. What continents are missing on this picture?

    a. North America, South America
    b. Europe, South America
    c. Africa, North America
    d. Australia, Asia, Antarctica

2. Where are the missing continents?

    a. on the inside of the globe
    b. on the bottom and other side of the globe
    c. beside the globe
    d. on top of the globe

3. Find the equator on the globe. The places near the equator are very hot. Name two continents that touch the equator.

    _____

Geography

Name:_____ **Date:**_____

Directions: Read the text, and look at the map. Answer the questions.

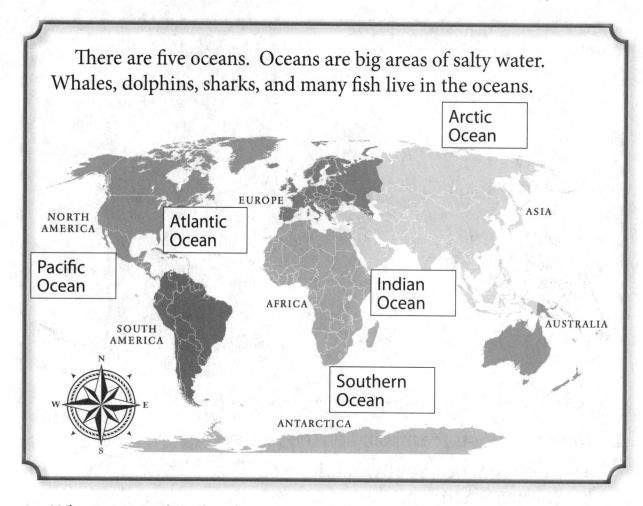

There are five oceans. Oceans are big areas of salty water. Whales, dolphins, sharks, and many fish live in the oceans.

Arctic Ocean

EUROPE

ASIA

NORTH AMERICA

Atlantic Ocean

Pacific Ocean

Indian Ocean

AFRICA

SOUTH AMERICA

AUSTRALIA

Southern Ocean

ANTARCTICA

N

W   E

S

1. What oceans border the east and west coasts of the United States?

    a. Southern Ocean and Indian Ocean

    b. Pacific Ocean and Atlantic Ocean

    c. Atlantic Ocean and Arctic Ocean

    d. Pacific Ocean and Indian Ocean

2. What else do you know about the oceans?

_____

_____

_____

51394—180 Days of Social Studies

© Shell Education

Name: _____ **Date:** _____

Directions: Follow the steps to finish this map.

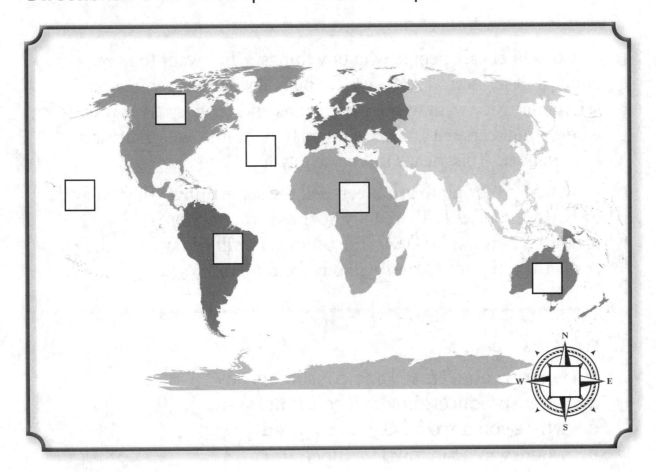

1. Add the following to the map:

   - Number **1**: Pacific Ocean
   - Number **2**: Atlantic Ocean
   - Number **3**: the compass rose
   - Number **4**: North America
   - Number **5**: South America
   - Number **6**: Africa
   - Number **7**: Australia

2. Color the oceans blue.

3. Put a star where you live.

Economics

Name:_____ **Date:**_____

Directions: Read the text, and answer the questions.

> Consumers are people who buy things. They want to have goods and services. Producers are people who make things and sell them. They want to sell their goods and services. A *market* is where producers sell and consumers buy. Your town or city is a *local market*. This means it is close to you.
>
> Often, two or more producers sell the same thing. There may be two pizza places. There may be three grocery stores. This means there is *competition*. The producers will all try to be the best. Then, the consumers will buy from them.

1. What is a market?

   a. where producers sell and consumers buy
   b. where producers buy and consumers sell
   c. where you go to have your car fixed
   d. where you go in town for lunch

2. Based on the text, where is a local market?

   a. far away
   b. in another country
   c. in another state
   d. close to you

3. What happens when two or more producers sell the same thing?

   a. They all work together.
   b. They compete.
   c. They go to school.
   d. They move away.

© *Shell Education*

Name:_____ **Date:**_____

Directions: Look at the pictures, and read the text. Answer the questions.

Economics

Mary's Bakery makes breads, cakes, and cookies. People like the bakery. They buy its goods. Mary serves tea, coffee, and milk. The bakery has been open for many years. It has made the same recipes since it opened.

Sammy's Bakery has just opened. Sammy makes breads, cakes, cookies, and muffins. He serves tea, coffee, milk, and juice. There is a big poster in the window. It says, "Buy a muffin and get a free drink." Each day, there are new flavors of muffins.

1. What are Mary and Sammy?

   a. truckers   **c.** teachers
   b. producers   **d.** librarians

2. What does Sammy sell that is different from Mary?

   a. coffee and tea   **c.** muffins and juice
   b. breads and cakes   **d.** milk and cakes

3. Who do you think will sell more goods? Why?

_____

_____

Economics

Name:_____   **Date:**_____

Directions: Look at the infographic. Answer the questions.

Ellie went to the market. She likes to make the best deals possible.

1. Mr. Green sells bread for $2. Mrs. Little sells bread for $1.
    Mrs. Sunshine sells bread for $3. Which one will Ellie buy?

    a. Mr. Green's bread   **c.** Mrs. Sunshine's bread
    b. Mrs. Little's bread   **d.** Mr. Peters' bread

2. Ellie wants to get some eggs. Mr. Green sells 12 eggs for $3.
    Mrs. Little sells 12 eggs for $4. Mrs. Sunshine sells 12 eggs for $4.
    But if you buy 2 cartons of eggs, she will sell them for $2 each.
    Which eggs will Ellie buy?

    a. Mr. Green's eggs for $3
    b. Mrs. Little's eggs for $4
    c. Mrs. Sunshine's eggs for $4
    d. Mrs. Sunshine's eggs: 2 boxes

3. Ellie brought jars of her mom's jam to trade. Mrs. Sunshine will
    trade 10 cookies for a jar of jam. Mr. Green will trade 15 muffins for
    a jar of jam. Which trade will Ellie make? Why?

    _____

    _____

51394—180 Days of Social Studies

© Shell Education

Name: _____ **Date:** _____

Directions: Read the table. Answer the questions.

Wilton Mall		Belmont Mall	
sweater	$10	sweater	$12
pants	$15	pants	$20
shoes	$20	shoes	$18
puzzle	$8	puzzle	$6

1. You want to buy new shoes. You go to the Wilton Mall. Then, you go to the Belmont Mall. You compare the prices. Which shoes will you buy?

   a. shoes at Wilton Mall   **c.** shoes at both malls
   b. shoes at Belmont Mall   **d.** boots at both malls

2. You are going to buy pants and a puzzle. At which mall will you buy each item? Why?

   _____

3. When you shop with your family, do you compare prices? Why?

   _____

   _____

Economics

Name:_____ **Date:**_____

Directions: Match each word in the first column to the correct meaning.

trade	It is where producers sell and consumers buy.
consumers	All the producers try to be the best. They want the consumer to buy their product.
producers	Two people have goods. They change one for the other. They do not buy the goods with money.
market	They make and sell goods and services.
competition	The actions or jobs that producers do.
goods	They buy goods and services.
services	These are the things that we buy.

51394—180 Days of Social Studies

© Shell Education

Name: _____ **Date:** _____

Directions: Look at the picture, and read the text. Answer the questions.

Louis Pasteur was a famous scientist. He lived in France many years ago. He and his wife had five children. Three of them died from a disease called *typhoid*. After that, Pasteur wanted to learn about diseases. He studied germs. He learned they are living things. He learned if you boil liquids, such as milk, it will kill germs. Then, they are safe to drink. This is called *pasteurization*. He learned how to make a *vaccine*. It would help people not get diseases, such as rabies. Today, tools for surgery are heated to kill germs. Pasteur's work helped save lives.

1. Why did Pasteur want to learn about diseases?

   a. Two of his friends had a disease.

   b. Three of his children died of a disease.

   c. He had five children.

   d. Four scientists told him to.

2. How did Pasteur make liquids safe to drink?

   a. He froze them to kill germs.

   b. He made a vaccine.

   c. He boiled them to kill germs.

   d. He learned they are living things.

3. How did Pasteur save people from diseases?

   a. He learned to kill germs.

   b. He made drinks safe.

   c. He learned to make a vaccine.

   d. all of the above

History

Name:_____ **Date:**_____

Directions: Look at the picture, and read the text. Answer the questions.

FIRST: Golda Meir was born in a place called the Ukraine. There was a war. It was dangerous for Jewish people. Her family moved to Wisconsin.

NEXT: When she was 23, she moved to the place now known as Israel. She worked for the government. She wanted people to have better houses. She wanted them to have better jobs. She wanted to help build the State of Israel. In 1948, Israel became a country.

THEN: Meir was the first female prime minister of Israel. She was a very strong person. She helped her country win a war.

1. Why did Meir's family move to the United States?

    a. They were in Israel.

    b. They went on vacation.

    c. It was a happy time.

    d. It was dangerous in the Ukraine.

2. What did Meir want to do in Israel?

    a. to help children and be a teacher

    b. to help build the State of Israel

    c. to help people and build houses

    d. to help children and be a doctor

© Shell Education

Name: _____ **Date:** _____

Directions: Look at the infographic, and answer the questions.

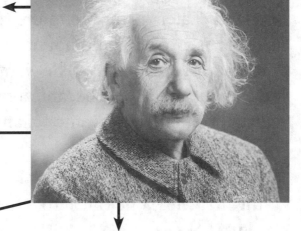

1
Albert Einstein did not like school. His teachers said he would never do anything good. But he loved math and science.

2
When he grew up, he was a math and science teacher.

3
Einstein's Theory of Relativity says when things move very fast, they look shorter.

4
His ideas helped other scientists invent nuclear energy. He won the Nobel Prize.

History

1. Which came first?

    a. Einstein's ideas helped other scientists.

    b. Einstein was a math and science teacher.

    c. Einstein was famous for his theory.

    d. Einstein did not like school.

2. What happens to things when they move very fast?

    a. They look shorter.

    b. They look longer.

    c. They look wider.

    d. They look thinner.

3. How did Einstein help other people?

_____

_____

History

Name: _____ Date: _____

Directions: Look at the picture, and read the text. Answer the questions.

Alexander Graham Bell grew up in Scotland. Later, he moved to the United States. His mother could not hear. His wife was deaf, too. And so he wanted to learn about sound. He became a teacher and an inventor. He invented many things to help people.

- He invented the telephone. He made the first telephone call across the United States.

- He invented the metal detector. He used it to find metal in things.

- He invented the audiometer. It helped him to see who had hearing problems.

1. Who was Alexander Graham Bell?

   a. a famous doctor   c. a deaf person
   b. a famous inventor   d. a famous teacher

2. Do you use a thing that was invented by Bell? Tell about it.

   _____

   _____

   _____

   _____

51394—180 Days of Social Studies   © *Shell Education*

Name: _____   **Date:** _____

Directions: Why are these people famous? Tell what you learned.

Why Are They Famous?	
 Pasteur	He was a famous _____. He learned about _____. He learned how to make a _____.
 Meir	She helped build the State of _____. She was the first woman _____ _____ of Israel.
 Einstein	He was famous for his _____ of _____. His ideas helped scientists invent _____ _____.
 Bell	He was an _____. He invented the _____.

Civics

Name:_____ **Date:**_____

Directions: Look at the picture, and read the text. Answer the questions.

Rules help us to be good citizens. They keep us happy and safe. They teach us to show respect and to be kind. Rules help us know what to do and what not to do.

At home, our parents make the rules. In class, the teacher makes the rules.

Rules have to be clear so everyone understands them. Rules need to be fair for everyone. If we do not follow a rule, there may be consequences. Our parents will talk to us. Our teacher will talk to us. They will tell us why we must follow the rule.

1. Which one is *not* true?

   a. Rules keep us happy and safe.
   b. Rules teach us to show respect.
   c. Rules are not important.
   d. Rules remind us to be kind.

2. What do rules have to be?

   a. silly and funny   **c.** just made up for fun
   b. clear and fair   **d.** changing all the time

3. What happens if we do not follow rules?

   a. We may get a yummy treat.
   b. We may get a nice reward.
   c. We may get to do it again.
   d. We may have a consequence.

Name: _____ **Date:** _____

Directions: Look at the picture, and read the text. Answer the questions.

Our community has rules. We call them laws. Laws help us to be good citizens. They keep us safe. They tell us what we can or cannot do. Traffic laws keep us safe on our streets. We know when to walk or when to wait. We wear our seat belts.

People in our government make laws. Everyone must follow them. Laws need to be clear so we understand them. They need to be fair for everyone. If we do not follow a law, something will happen. There will be a consequence.

1. Why do we have laws in our communities?

   a. so we will eat our vegetables

   b. so we will be protected

   c. so we can do whatever we want

   d. so we will do our homework

2. Who must follow laws?

   a. only children   **c.** all people

   b. only parents   **d.** only teachers

3. Look at the picture. What law are the children following?

   _____

   _____

Civics

Name:_____ **Date:**_____

Directions: Look at the infographic, and answer the questions.

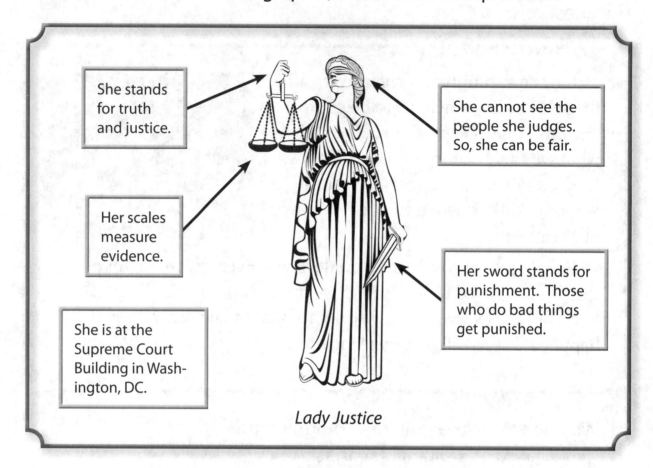

She stands for truth and justice.

She cannot see the people she judges. So, she can be fair.

Her scales measure evidence.

Her sword stands for punishment. Those who do bad things get punished.

She is at the Supreme Court Building in Washington, DC.

Lady Justice

1. What does Lady Justice stand for?

   a. truth and justice   **c.** strength and love
   b. peace and love   **d.** peace and strength

2. Why does she have a blindfold?

   a. She can see under it.   **c.** She wants to be fair.
   b. She is playing a game. **d.** She wants to hide.

3. Why does Lady Justice have a sword? What will happen to those who do bad things?

   _____

   _____

                    © *Shell Education*

Name:_____ **Date:**_____

Directions: Look at the pictures, and read the text. Answer the questions.

1. In the first picture, what rule are the children following?

   a. We play when it's work time.
   b. We put away our toys.
   c. We raise our hand to speak.
   d. We run around in class.

2. What law do you obey when you sit in a car?

   a. play with the steering wheel
   b. put the window down
   c. sit in the front seat
   d. wear a seat belt

3. Tell about two other rules or laws that you obey each day. Why do you obey them?

   _____

   _____

Civics

Name: _____   Date: _____

Directions: Read the text. Write **R** for the ones that are rules. Write **L** for the ones that are laws.

R or L?	Rule or Law
	We work quietly in class.
	We stop at a stop sign.
	We do not steal.
	We do not run in the hallway.
	We do not litter in the park.
	We do not fight with others.
	We do not hurt dogs or cats.
	We go to school every day.
	We keep our hands and feet to ourselves.
	We clean up our toys.

51394—180 Days of Social Studies

© Shell Education

Name: _____ **Date:** _____

Directions: Read the text, and look at the picture. Answer the questions.

Many people come to the United States from different places. They are called *immigrants*. They bring their food recipes. Yum! In Germany, many people eat sausages. In France, people eat pastries. Here are some more foods you might like:

- pizza—comes from Italy
- fried chicken—comes from Scotland
- apple pie—comes from England
- peanut butter—comes from South America

In our communities, we have restaurants. We can eat foods from other places. There are many different flavors.

1. Where does apple pie come from?

   a. France   **c.** England

   b. Italy   **d.** Germany

2. Which one is *not* true?

   a. Pizza comes from Italy.

   b. Fried chicken comes from Germany.

   c. Peanut butter comes from South America.

   d. Sausages come from Germany.

3. What is a good reason for going to restaurants with foods from other places?

   _____

   _____

Geography

Name: _____ Date:_____

Directions: Read the text, and look at the map. Answer the questions.

The United States is a very big country. Immigrants bring their languages from their old countries. They also bring their music. They bring their religions. Many of us are immigrants. Or, our moms and dads are immigrants. This makes the United States an interesting place!

Long ago, people came here from Spain. They settled in this country. That is why today, many of us still speak Spanish. We speak Chinese, French, and German, too. And more!

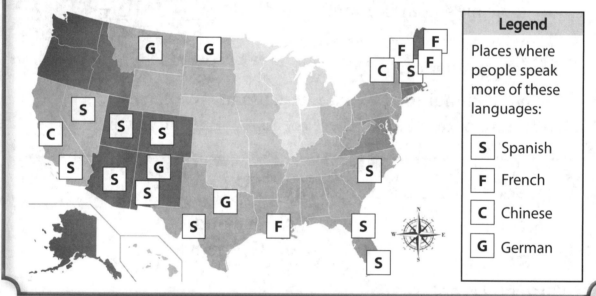

Legend

Places where people speak more of these languages:

S Spanish
F French
C Chinese
G German

1. We speak English in all states. After English, what language do we speak the most in the southern United States?

   a. French
   b. German
   c. Chinese
   d. Spanish

2. Find your state on the map. What do people speak in your state? What languages do you speak?

_____

_____

Name: _____ **Date:** _____

Directions: Look at the map, and answer the questions.

1. Where is the gas station near?

   a. the mountains   **c.** the houses
   b. the market   **d.** the Ferris wheel

2. Write **P** on the things that are made by people. Write **N** on the things that are made by nature.

3. What do you have in your community that is *not* on this map?

   _____

   _____

   _____

Geography

Name:_____ **Date:**_____

Directions: Look at the pictures, and read the text. Answer the questions.

There are places that make our community interesting. We go fishing in the creek. We go shopping at stores. We climb and play at the park. We watch baseball games at the stadium. We see dinosaur fossils at the museum. We watch airplanes at the airport. We eat at restaurants. We learn at school.

 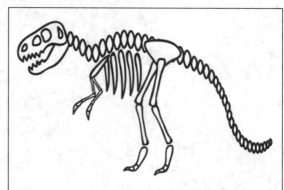

1. What can we do at the museum?

   a. go shopping   **c.** see dinosaur fossils

   b. go fishing   **d.** watch airplanes

2. Where can we go to go fishing?

   a. the museum   **c.** the airport

   b. the stadium   **d.** the creek

3. What things can you do in your community?

   _____

   _____

   _____

51394—180 Days of Social Studies
© Shell Education

Name:_____ **Date:**_____

Directions: Look at the community map. Answer the questions.

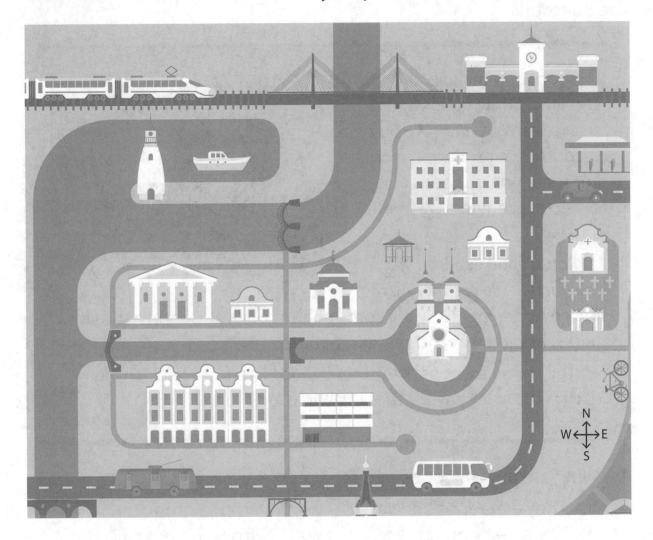

1. Circle these places on the map:
    - lighthouse
    - clock tower
    - bus
    - hospital
    - bridge

2. Write **P** on all of the things that are made by people.

3. Write **N** on the things that are made by nature.

Economics

Name:_____ Date:_____

Directions: Look at the picture, and read the text. Answer the questions.

Producers make goods and services. Some goods and services are *private*. We buy them from a producer. Here are some private goods and services: a movie, a pet, books, and gas.

Some goods and services are *public*. We get them from the government. Here are some public goods and services: roads, parks, bridges, street signs, and police.

The government pays for these goods and services. We pay taxes. The taxes pay for these public goods and services.

1. What are private goods and services?

   a. They are goods and services we buy from a producer.
   b. They are goods and services we buy from the police.
   c. They are goods and services we buy from a school.
   d. They are goods and services we buy from the government.

2. Which one is *not* a public good or service?

   a. road   **c.** movie
   b. police   **d.** street sign

3. How does the government pay for goods and services?

   a. with police   **c.** with parks
   b. with roads   **d.** with taxes

© *Shell Education*

Name:_____ **Date:**_____

Directions: Look at the pictures, and read the text. Answer the questions.

These officers work for the city. They keep people safe. We are happy they help us.

1. Who pays an officer to work in the city?

    a. their parents
    b. the city government
    c. a store in the city
    d. a factory in the city

2. What kind of work do officers do?

    a. They teach in a school.
    b. They sell in a store.
    c. They clean in a hospital.
    d. They do a service.

3. Look at the picture. What goods do you see?

    a. trees and land
    b. sky and birds
    c. uniforms and patches
    d. groceries and toys

Economics

Name: _____ **Date:** _____

Directions: Look at the picture, and answer the questions.

1. Here is a classroom. Who is doing a public service?

   a. the desks   **c.** the boards
   b. the students   **d.** the teacher

2. What goods were paid for by the government?

   _____

   _____

3. Name three other people who work in a school. Who pays for their services?

   _____

   _____

51394—180 Days of Social Studies   © Shell Education

Name: _____ **Date:** _____

Directions: Look at the pictures. Answer the questions.

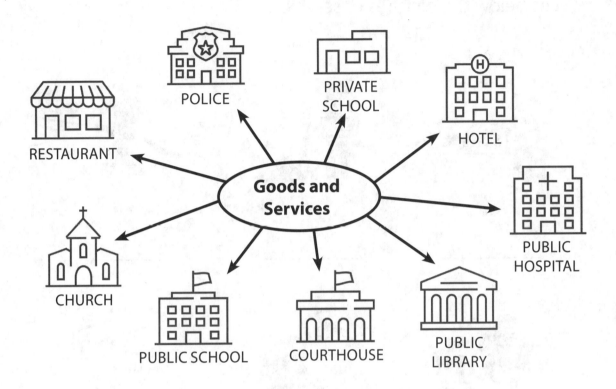

1. You are not feeling well. You have a fever. Which public service can help you?

    a. the public school   **c.** the public hospital
    b. the public library   **d.** the courthouse

2. Look at the pictures. Circle the public goods and services.

3. Think about where you live. List three goods and services paid for by the government.

    _____

    _____

    _____

Name:_____ **Date:**_____

Directions: Write **G** for goods below the pictures of goods. Write **S** for services below the pictures of services.

Economics

_____ _____ _____

_____ _____ _____

_____ _____ _____

51394—180 Days of Social Studies
© Shell Education

Name:_____ **Date:**_____

Directions: Read the text. Answer the questions.

> A long time ago, family life was different. There were many children in each family. There were no computers or cars. Everyone in the family had a job.
>
> Moms and dads worked at home. Mothers made the food and the clothes. They made candles to burn for light. Fathers built the house and the barn. They took care of the farm animals. The cows gave milk, and the chickens gave eggs. Sometimes, fathers hunted or fished. Both parents planted the crops in the fields.
>
> Children helped their parents grow and make things. Everyone worked hard.

1. How was life different a long time ago?
   a. There were only a few children in each family.
   b. No one in the family had jobs to do at home.
   c. Mother worked far away from home.
   d. There were no computers and cars.

2. What would have happened if there were no farm animals, gardens, or crops? Circle all that apply.
   a. The children would not have a pet.
   b. Boys and girls would not have to work.
   c. Dad could not hunt or fish.
   d. There would be little or no food for the family.

3. Why do you think everyone had a job?
   a. Everyone liked to work.
   b. There was nothing better to do.
   c. Everything had to be grown or made.
   d. Parents were ill.

History

Name: _____ **Date:** _____

Directions: Look at the picture, and read the text. Answer the questions.

Some things could not be made on the farm. Mom and dad could buy them at the general store. They bought things such as cloth, pots, tools, boots, or lanterns. They put these things in a sack, a basket, or a wooden box.

1. What could you buy at the store long ago?

   a. hammer and nails
   b. frozen meal
   c. computer
   d. gas for the car

2. How did you carry what you bought?

   a. in a plastic bag
   b. in a cardboard box
   c. in the trunk of the car
   d. in a basket or a sack

3. How can the picture help you learn about life long ago?

   _____

   _____

Name:_____ **Date:**_____

Directions: Look at the pictures, and answer the questions.

building a house long ago

building a house today

1. How did people build a house long ago?

   a. They built it very quickly.

   b. They built it slowly and made what they needed.

   c. They used machines to build the house.

   d. They built the house on cement.

2. How do people build a house today?

   a. They start on the top of the house.

   b. They build it slowly, placing each piece by hand.

   c. They make everything they need.

   d. They use machines and buy what they need.

3. Would you rather build a house long ago or today? Why?

   _____

   _____

   _____

   _____

© Shell Education

History

Name: _____ **Date:** _____

Directions: Look at the picture, and read the text. Answer the questions.

This picture shows a one-room schoolhouse from long ago. The children learned to read, write, and work with numbers. They did what the teacher said. The class could have children of many ages.

1. How is this school different from yours?

   a. It has books for students to read.
   b. It has desks for students to sit at.
   c. It has slates for students to write on.
   d. It has a door.

2. How is this school the same as yours?

   _____

   _____

3. Would you rather go to school long ago or today? Why?

   _____

   _____

© Shell Education

Name:_____   **Date:**_____

Directions: Read Anna's diary. She is eight years old. Compare your life to hers by filling in the Venn diagram.

Dear Diary,

I got up at five o'clock. Ma made breakfast in a pan over the fire. Pa went to milk the cow.

It was seven o'clock. It was time for school. We walked two miles. My sisters are in the same class as I am.

At school, we read our books. We wrote on our slates. We listened to the teacher. We did not want to sit in the corner!

Later, we swept the floor and wiped the boards. Then, it was time to go.

At home, I was tired, but I helped Ma with chores. Pa was planting in the field. Ma made a yummy stew for supper. We ate homemade bread, too. Then, we did our homework. Ma lit a candle so we could see.

Time for bed. I climbed the ladder to the loft. Goodnight!

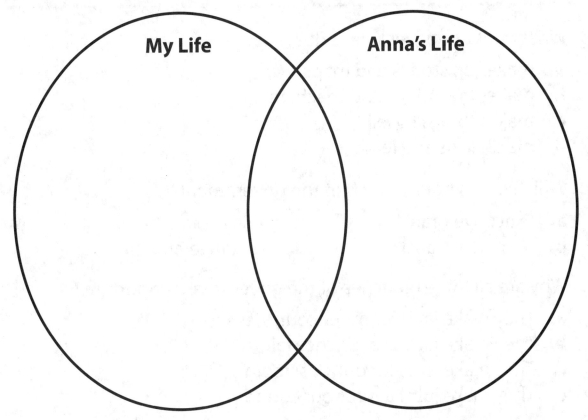

My Life   Anna's Life

Civics

Name: _____ **Date:** _____

Directions: Look at the picture, and read the text. Answer the questions.

> Our government is made up of citizens. They work for our community, our state, and our country. They make laws. They make decisions. They lead.
>
> Our government has three branches:
> - The legislative branch makes the laws.
> - The executive branch makes sure the laws are applied.
> - The judicial branch makes sure the laws are just. They punish people who break the laws.
>
> The three branches are all important. People from our government make the laws, apply the laws, and make sure they are just. They do this for our city, our state, and our country.

1. What does our government do?
   a. makes up stories and maps
   b. makes inventions and machines
   c. makes things to sell
   d. makes laws and leads

2. Which one is not a branch of the government?
   a. executive branch
   b. monarch branch
   c. judicial branch
   d. legislative branch

3. Why are all three branches of the government important?
   a. They make laws for other countries.
   b. They make laws that are not fair.
   c. They make rules for our classroom.
   d. They make just laws for our country.

51394—180 Days of Social Studies

© Shell Education

Name: _____ **Date:** _____

Directions: Look at the picture, and read the text. Answer the questions.

The president is the leader of our country. The president is the leader of the executive branch. The president is the leader of the military, too.

Congress writes the laws. Then, the president signs the laws and makes sure the laws are applied. The president can veto, or stop, a law.

The president chooses people to work for the cabinet and other offices. The president meets with important people.

1. Who is the president?

   a. person who works for the leader of our country
   b. person who is the leader of our country
   c. person who wants to be the leader of our country
   d. person who knows the leader of our country

2. Who is the leader of the executive branch?

   a. the vice president
   b. Congress
   c. the president
   d. the cabinet

3. Which one is *not* a job the president does?

   a. signs the laws
   b. chooses people for the cabinet
   c. meets important people
   d. writes the laws

© Shell Education

Civics

Name: _____ **Date:** _____

Directions: Look at the infographic. Answer the questions.

helps the president

stands in for the president if something happens

can break a tie in the Senate

is in the executive branch

1. What does the vice president do?
   a. stands in for the president
   b. breaks a tie for the Senate
   c. works in the executive branch
   d. all the above

2. Look at the picture. What symbols are *not* on the seal?
   a. an eagle
   b. a duck
   c. a shield
   d. an olive branch

3. Why is the vice president's job important?

   _____

   _____

   _____

© Shell Education

Name: _____ **Date:** _____

Directions: Look at the picture, and read the text. Answer the questions.

Our president is the leader of our country. Our vice president helps the president lead. Leaders have many good traits.

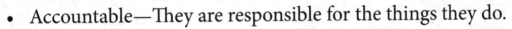

- Honest—They tell the truth.
- Respectful—They respect and care for the people.
- Accountable—They are responsible for the things they do.
- Wise—They have experience and know right from wrong.
- Responsible—They work hard. They keep their promises.
- Compassionate—They understand when the people need their help.

1. Which one is *not* true?

   a. A good leader is accountable.
   b. A good leader is not honest.
   c. A good leader shows respect.
   d. A good leader shows compassion.

2. If you were the president, how would you show respect for the people?

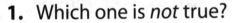

_____

_____

_____

Civics

Name: _____ Date: _____

Directions: Read the text, and answer the question.

The President...	The Vice President...
• is the leader of our country • is the leader of the executive branch • is the leader of the military • signs the laws • makes sure the laws are applied • can veto a law • chooses people to work for the cabinet and other offices • meets with important people • works and lives in the White House • serves for four or eight years	• is in the executive branch • helps the president for four or eight years • stands in if something happens to the president • will vote in the Senate if there is a tie • has an office in the west wing of the White House

1. The president and the vice president do very important jobs for our country. How are their jobs the same? How are they different?

_____

_____

_____

_____

_____

_____

51394—180 Days of Social Studies

© Shell Education

Name: _____ **Date:** _____

Directions: Read the text, and look at the map. Answer the questions.

In some places, it is cold in the winter. Look at the map. Where is it colder? Is it colder in the north or in the south? We get snow in the north. We wear warm clothes.

In some states, it is warm all year round. Look at the map. It is warmer in the south. We wear light clothes all year.

In some places, it is wet or dry. If we have more rain, we can grow food. If we have warm weather, we can grow more kinds of foods. We can grow oranges and lemons in Florida. We cannot grow them in the north.

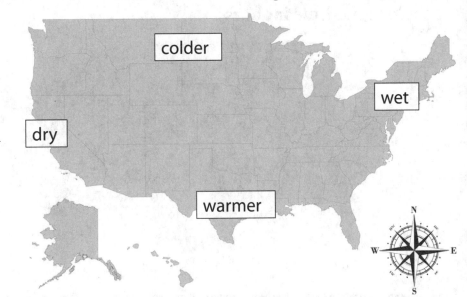

1. Based on the text, what can we do in cold weather?

   a. grow many kinds of food
   b. wear light clothes
   c. grow oranges
   d. wear warm clothes

2. Where would you find more rain?

   a. in the north states
   b. in the south states
   c. in the east states
   d. in the west states

Name: _____ **Date:** _____

Geography

Directions: Read the text, and look at the map. Answer the questions.

It is cold high in the mountains. There is snow. People can ski or snowboard there.

Some communities are near water. They can be near an ocean. They can be near a lake or a river. People can swim there. They can boat and water-ski, too.

The weather can change each day. It can be sunny or cloudy. Then, people enjoy the outdoors. It can rain or storm. Then, people spend time indoors.

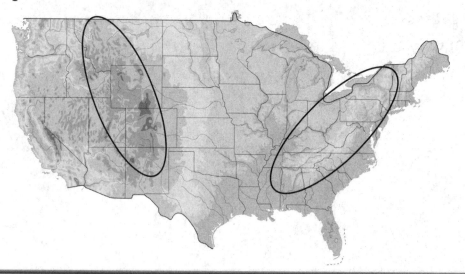

1. What three things can people do if they live near water?

   a. swim in an ocean   c. walk in a desert
   b. boat in a lake   d. water-ski on a river

2. What is it like high in the mountains?

   a. It is warm.   c. It is hot.
   b. It is wet.   d. It is cold.

3. What is the weather like where you live?

   _____

Name:_____ **Date:**_____

Directions: Look at the pictures, and read the text. Answer the questions.

1. Where do people build *most* towns and cities?

   a. on mountains   **c.** on flat land
   b. on the water   **d.** on a glacier

2. Why do you think people build near water?

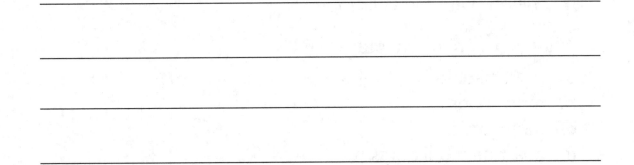

Name: _____ **Date:** _____

Geography

Directions: Look at the pictures, and read the text. Answer the questions.

Some people live in a place that is rural. They do not live in a city. There are not as many people as in a city. There are more forests. There are farms and farm animals. There are not as many houses. There are not as many roads or stores. It is quieter.

Some people live in a place that is urban. They live in a town or city. There are more people. There are more buildings. There are more houses and apartments. There can be skyscrapers. There are more roads. There is more noise.

1. Look at the pictures. Which one shows an urban area?

    a. the one with the houses
    b. the one with the barn and cows
    c. the one with the river
    d. the one with the skyscrapers

2. What do you find in a rural area?

    a. more people
    b. more roads
    c. more forests
    d. apartment buildings

51394—180 Days of Social Studies
© Shell Education

Name: _____ **Date:** _____

Directions: Look at the pictures, and read the text. Complete the chart.

What can you do if …	
…you live near the mountains?	
…it is winter, and you live in the north?	
…you live in a rural area?	
…it is raining, and you want to play?	

Geography

109

Economics

Name:_____   Date:_____

Directions: Read the text, and answer the questions.

> *Scarcity* is when there is not enough of something. There are not enough goods or services. Many people want a good or service. Only some can have it. People might want more than they can get.
>
> We use *resources* to make goods and services. Money is a resource, too. When there are not enough resources, we have scarcity.

Scarcity
• We need more resources.
• We need more money.
• We need more workers.

Resources		
gas	oil	electricity
water	trees	cotton
wool	workers	money

1. What is scarcity?

   a. There are too many goods.

   b. There are too many services.

   c. There are too many workers.

   d. There are not enough goods.

2. Which one is *not* a resource?

   a. electricity   c. a service

   b. workers   d. money

3. Circle the three that are true. Scarcity happens if we need more

   a. resources.   c. money.

   b. school.   d. workers.

51394—180 Days of Social Studies

© Shell Education

Name: _____ **Date:** _____

Directions: Look at the pictures, and read the text. Answer the questions.

Reese was playing in a soccer game. Dad said, "Work hard at the game and you will get a treat!" Reese practiced a lot and played really well. She passed the ball and scored a goal.

Dad said, "Great! Here is one dollar so you can buy a treat."

They drove to the store on the way home. Reese wanted a juice and a candy bar. Each one cost one dollar, so she asked her dad for one dollar more.

He replied, "Sorry, Reese. I only have one dollar with me, so you will have to choose."

Since she was very thirsty, Reese decided to buy the juice.

1. What did Reese want?

   a. soccer and candy   **c.** a juice and a candy bar
   b. candy and a toy   **d.** a toy and a candy bar

2. What did her dad say when Reese asked for more money?

   a. "Yes, here is more."   **c.** "You played a good game."
   b. "It's time to go home." **d.** "I only have one dollar."

3. What did Reese decide?

   a. to have the candy bar   **c.** to have both
   b. to have the juice   **d.** to have neither

Economics

Name: _____ **Date:** _____

Directions: Look at the picture, and read the text. Answer the questions.

We have many
- desks,
- tables,
- books,
- cupboards, and
- boards.

We do not have
- paper towels,
- dish soap, and
- tissues.

1. What three things are *not* scarce in the class?

   a. desks
   b. tables

   c. dish soap
   d. books

2. What is scarce in the classroom?

   _____

   _____

3. How will the teacher solve the problem?

   _____

   _____

51394—180 Days of Social Studies

© Shell Education

Name:_____ **Date:**_____

Directions: Look at the pictures, and read the text. Answer the questions. Solve the problems.

1	2	3
Four children sat at the table. They were drawing, cutting, and pasting. There were only two pairs of scissors. What would you do?	The children lined up. They waited for their lunch. When it was Lilly's turn, there was no chocolate milk left. What would you do?	Robin wanted two cookies and a glass of milk. She poured the milk. Then, she looked in the cookie jar. There were two cookies. Robin's little brother asked for one. What would you do?

1. Read text box **1**. What would you do?

    a. Take a pair of scissors and use them for yourself.

    b. Take a pair of scissors and hide them.

    c. Use a pair of scissors, but then share them.

    d. You would not finish the drawing.

2. Read text box **2**. How would you solve the problem?

    _____

    _____

3. Read text box **3**. Think of two ways to solve the problem.

    _____

    _____

Economics

Name:_____ **Date:**_____

Directions: Read the newspaper article. There is some bad advice in it. Circle the six correct ideas that can help the town save water.

Scarcity of Water in Smalltown!

It has been a very hot and dry summer in Smalltown again this year. There has not been enough rain. Water is scarce. The grass is dry. The flowers are dying. The weather forecaster is taking a holiday. Everyone is sad. What can be done? How can we save water? Here is some advice.

The mayor says, "No more water for the lawns."

Take lots of baths. Fill the tub to the top.

Let the water run when you brush your teeth.

Do not take a long shower.

Use a rain barrel to collect the little bit of rain water.

Water the lawn every day.

Use recycled water for the yard.

Do not wash your car so often.

Plant gardens that do not need so much water.

© Shell Education

Name: _____ **Date:** _____

Directions: Look at the picture, and read the text. Answer the questions.

History

Maria Tallchief was the first top American Indian ballet dancer. She was from the Osage Nation in Oklahoma. Tallchief started to dance when she was three years old. She studied ballet for many years and practiced every day. When she grew up, she danced in cities all over the world. Tallchief danced in New York City and in Paris. She danced for the American Ballet. She started a ballet company in Chicago. She won many awards. Then, she became a ballet teacher. Now, other American Indians want to be ballet dancers like Tallchief.

1. When did Tallchief start ballet?

   a. when she was four years old
   b. when she was six years old
   c. when she was seven years old
   d. when she was three years old

2. Where did she dance?

   a. in cities all over the world
   b. in schools all over the country
   c. on farms all over the world
   d in stores all over the world

3. What did she start in Chicago?

   a. the New York Ballet   c. a ballet company
   b. the American Ballet   d. the Paris Ballet

History

Name:_____ Date:_____

Directions: Look at the picture, and read the text. Answer the questions.

Will Rogers was part Cherokee. He was born in Oklahoma and grew up on a ranch. When he was little, he learned to ride a horse and use a lasso. When he got older, he was an actor in movies. Rogers was also a cowboy. He could do trick horse riding. He was a writer and comedian. People listened to him on the radio. They thought he was funny and smart. He talked about how to help people. Rogers traveled all over the world. Many people liked to listen to him. Today, people like to read his books.

1. What did Rogers learn when he was a little boy?

   a. to write a book
   b. to be an actor
   c. to be a comedian
   d. to ride and lasso

2. Rogers was an actor. What else did he do?

   a. He was a teacher and a librarian.
   b. He was a cowboy and a writer.
   c. He was lawyer and a painter.
   d. He was a doctor and a scientist.

3. Based on the text, why did many people like to listen to him?

   a. He was happy and talked about riding a horse.
   b. He was funny and talked about helping people.
   c. He was happy and talked about using a lasso.
   d. He was funny and talked about being a clown.

51394—180 Days of Social Studies   © Shell Education

Name: _____ **Date:** _____

Directions: Look at the pictures. Answer the questions.

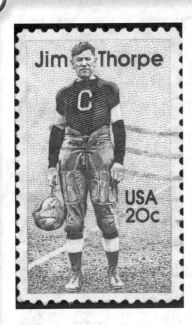

Jim Thorpe, an American
Indian

1. Who was Jim Thorpe?

   a. a famous athlete   **c.** a famous doctor

   b. a famous inventor   **d.** a famous lawyer

2. What are two sports that Thorpe played?

_____

_____

3. Thorpe won two gold medals at the Olympics. Why do you think this is important?

_____

_____

History

Name: _____ Date: _____

Directions: Look at the picture, and read the text. Answer the questions.

Pocahontas lived a long time ago. She was an American Indian. Her father was a chief. They lived near Jamestown, Virginia. Jamestown was an English community.

Sometimes, her people traded with the English. Sometimes, they would fight. One day, Captain John Smith was captured by her father's warriors. The chief was going to kill him! But Pocahontas saved him.

Later, the English took Pocahontas. They kept her prisoner for a long time. She married a farmer named John Rolfe. They went to England. Pocahontas changed her name and had a son. But she got very sick. She died in England.

1. Who was Pocahontas?

   a. She was an American Indian chief.
   b. She was the daughter of an English captain.
   c. She was the daughter of an American Indian chief.
   d. She was a captain.

2. What happened when the English took Pocahontas?

   _____

3. Why do you think Pocahontas is famous?

   _____

   _____

© Shell Education

Name:_____ **Date:**_____

Directions: What did you learn? Write one important thing for each person.

Maria Tallchief	Will Rogers

Famous American Indians

Pocahontas	Jim Thorpe

Civics

Name: _____ **Date:** _____

Directions: Look at the picture, and read the text. Answer the questions.

The United States has three levels of government. They are federal, state, and local. We vote for our leaders. They work for the citizens. They make decisions.

The federal level does many things. It writes laws for the country, such as laws for banks. It also prints money. The federal level makes trade laws with other countries. It can send the military to help people. The government may go to war with a country.

1. What are the three levels of government?

   a. upper, middle, lower
   b. local, state, federal
   c. executive, legislative, judicial
   d. Senate, representative, responsible

2. Who does the federal government work for?

   a. people from other countries
   b. some people in our country
   c. all citizens of our country
   d. the legislative branch

3. Which one is *not* true?

   a. The federal government writes laws for the country.
   b. The federal government prints money for the country.
   c. The federal government makes laws for banks in the country.
   d. The federal government makes laws for banks in other countries.

Name: _____ **Date:** _____

Directions: Read the text. Answer the questions.

Civics

Each state has a state government. We vote for a governor and representatives. The governor leads the state.

The governor ...
is in charge of the National Guard. It can help people in emergencies.
pardons prisoners. Then, the people can leave the prisons.
goes to special ceremonies or events.
applies laws for all of the people in the state.
works to have businesses and jobs in the state.
works with the representatives.
works with the president and the governors from other states.

1. Who is the governor?

   a. the leader of our country
   b. the leader of our city
   c. the leader of our state
   d. the leader of another country

2. Which one is *not* a job the governor does?

   a. applies laws for all the people of the state
   b. decides which laws are just in the state
   c. works to have businesses and jobs in the state
   d. is in charge of the National Guard

3. Who does the governor work with?

   a. Congress, the cabinet, the Senate
   b. the Senate, the House of Representatives
   c. representatives, governors, the president
   d. the cabinet, White House staff

Civics

Name:_____ **Date:**_____

Directions: Look at the pictures, and read the text. Answer the questions.

> The local government looks after many services.
>
>
>

1. Which one is *not* a local government service?

   a. running schools
   b. opening a public library
   c. cleaning town or city parks and trails
   d. printing money

2. What services does the local government look after in your community?

   _____

   _____

   _____

   _____

51394—180 Days of Social Studies

© Shell Education

Name: _____ **Date:** _____

Directions: Look at the picture, and read the text. Answer the questions.

Local government is in towns, cities, and counties. We vote for the mayor and the council. The mayor works at the town hall. In a city, the mayor works at the city hall.

The mayor and council pass laws for the community. Some services they look after are police, firefighters, houses, and transportation.

People can go to town meetings. They can see the mayor. They can say what they need. They say what their community needs.

1. Where is local government?

   a. country, state, city

   b. country, town, city

   c. towns, cities, counties

   d. state, country, town

2. Where would you go to tell the mayor what you need?

   a. White House meeting   **c.** town meeting

   b. court house meeting   **d.** library meeting

3. If you were mayor, what would you do for your community?

_____

_____

Civics

Name:_____ **Date:**_____

Directions: Write what you know about the federal government. Write what you know about the local government. How are they the same? How are they different?

Federal Government	Local Government
_____	_____
_____	_____
_____	_____

Same or Different?

_____

_____

_____

_____

51394—180 Days of Social Studies

© Shell Education

Name: _____ **Date:** _____

Directions: Look at the picture, and read the text. Answer the questions.

Long ago, people built their houses in villages. It was safe to live close together. They had family and friends close by. They helped each other.

Sometimes, the houses were built along a road. People traveled on the road to get from one place to another place. People sent goods from one place to another place along the road.

Some people used stone to build houses. Others built houses from wood where there were trees. They made log or wood houses. They also made tools from wood. They burned wood in fires or in stoves.

1. Based on the text, which one was *not* true long ago?

   a. Villages were safer.
   b. People lived close together.
   c. People liked to be far away.
   d. People helped each other.

2. What did they use to build houses?

   a. plastic and stone
   b. wood and stone
   c. straw and bone
   d. wood and plastic

Geography

Name:_____ Date:_____

Directions: Look at the picture, and read the text. Answer the questions.

Long ago, villages were built along the water. People traveled on boats to get from one place to another. They sent goods on boats, too. They ate fish from the lake, river, or ocean. They needed water to drink. They needed water for their crops. They lived where it sometimes rained. Crops did not grow in the desert areas.

1. Why were houses built along the water?

   a. It was warmer on the water.
   b. It was colder on the water.
   c. People traveled on the water.
   d. People traveled on the road.

2. Which one is *not* true?

   a. Houses were built along the water.
   b. People planted crops in the desert.
   c. People sent goods on boats.
   d. People needed water to drink.

3. What things might have made rivers hard to live close to?

   _____

   _____

51394—180 Days of Social Studies   © *Shell Education*

Name: _____ **Date:** _____

Directions: Look at the infographic. Answer the questions.

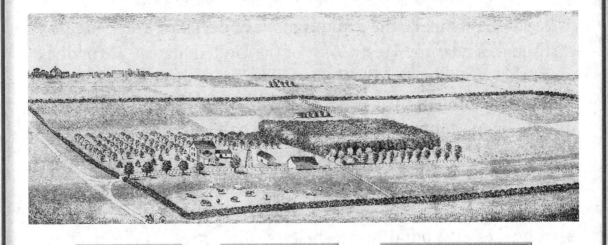

big farms—far apart for lots of crops

flat land—easy to build a house on or grow crops

clay soil— stays wet

sandy soil— stays dry

loam soil—good for crops

1. What kind of soil was good for planting crops?

    a. rocks   **c.** clay
    b. sand   **d.** loam

2. Why were farms far apart?

    a. The farmer could not plant crops.
    b. The farmer built his house on a mountain.
    c. The farmland was big.
    d. The farmland was cold.

3. Why did the farmer plant crops on flat land?

    _____

    _____

Geography

Name:_____ Date:_____

Directions: Read the text, and answer the questions.

> *Natural hazards* are dangerous. Earthquakes, tornadoes, and hurricanes are natural hazards. When they happen, people may get hurt, and buildings and crops may be damaged.
>
> Earthquakes make the ground move and shake. There are more earthquakes near the West Coast of the United States. Tornadoes make the wind blow hard. They spin and make funnels. Some break everything in their way. There are more tornadoes in the middle of our country. Hurricanes make the wind blow hard. It rains. Big waves from the ocean flood the land. There are more hurricanes near the East Coast.
>
> We build houses that can shake safely. They stay strong in earthquakes. We build storm shelters. They keep us safe in tornadoes. We build walls called breakers to stop the waves.

1. What happens when there is a natural hazard?

    a. People can get hurt.   **c.** People are happy.
    b. People can play games.   **d.** People celebrate.

2. What is a tornado?

    a. a place to visit
    b. a place where the ground shakes
    c. a big wind that makes a funnel
    d. a big wave from the ocean

3. Are there natural hazards that may happen where you live? Has a disaster happened before? Tell about where you live.

    _____

    _____

51394—180 Days of Social Studies

© *Shell Education*

Name: _____ **Date:** _____

Directions: Look at the pictures, and read the text. Answer the questions.

These can affect where people live:

- land
- roads
- water
- natural hazards

1. Circle the things in the pictures that are **good** for where people live. Place an **X** on the things that are **not good** for where people live.

2. Look at the things you have circled. Tell what you know about *one* of them.

_____

_____

_____

Economics

Name: _____ **Date:** _____

Directions: Read the text, and answer the questions.

Where do we get money? Most people work to earn money. They make goods. They offer services. They are workers.

People may get paid for each hour they work. They may get paid when a job is done. They may get paid the same amount of money each week.

People work at all kinds of jobs. They choose jobs for many reasons. They go to school to learn about the jobs. People may have the skills for the jobs. Most often, people need the money from the jobs.

1. Where do most people get money?

   a. Most people find money in their yards.
   b. Most people get money at school.
   c. Most people work to earn money.
   d. Most people get money in a game.

2. Which one is *not* true?

   a. People may get paid by the hour.
   b. People may get paid when a job is done.
   c. People may get paid by telephone.
   d. People may get the same amount each week.

3. Why do people choose the jobs where they work?

   a. They may like the jobs.
   b. They have the skills for the jobs.
   c. They need the money.
   d. all of the above

© Shell Education

Name: _____ **Date:** _____

Directions: Look at the pictures, and read the text. Answer the questions.

How do we know the work people do? We know what many workers do by the clothes they wear. They might have special tools. They study to learn about the job. They might talk about the things they know. Some people may learn from a person who is doing the job.

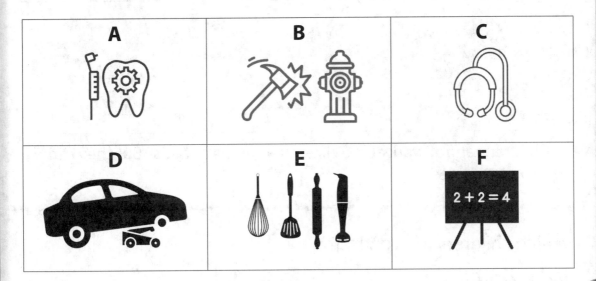

1. Who uses the **A** tool?

   a. teacher   **c.** dentist
   b. mechanic   **d.** firefighter

2. Which tools are used by a chef?

   a. A   **c.** D
   b. C   **d.** E

3. Where do you see the worker who uses the **F** tool?

   a. at the dentist's office   **c.** at home
   b. at school   **d.** at the doctor's office

Economics

Name: _____ **Date:** _____

Directions: Look at the pictures, and read the text. Answer the questions.

| 1 | 2 | 3 |
| 4 | 5 | 6 |

Children cannot work at jobs like their moms or dads. But they can get paid for chores.

1. Which children are working?

   a. 1, 2, 3, 4   **c.** 2, 3, 4, 5
   b. 2, 4, 5, 6   **d.** 3, 4, 5, 6

2. Which children will *not* get paid? Why not?

   _____

   _____

3. Which chores do you think may pay more? Why?

   _____

   _____

51394—180 Days of Social Studies   © Shell Education

Name:_____ **Date:**_____

Directions: Look at the pictures, and read the text. Answer the questions.

Feed the cat. $1	Wash the car. $10	Rake the leaves in the yard. $10
Wash the dinner dishes. $3	Clean your room. $3	Walk the dog. $2
Take the trash out to the curb. $2	Do your laundry. $5	Bring the groceries in from the car. $2

1. Reg washed the car, raked the leaves, and did his laundry. Why did he choose these chores?

   a. They look easy.   c. They pay more.
   b. They are outdoors.   d. They pay less.

2. Which jobs would you choose? Why?

_____

_____

_____

Economics

Name: _____ Date: _____

Directions: Read the text. Fill in the T-chart. Use the Word Bank to help you.

Who are the workers in your community?	What are some jobs you may want to do when you grow up?

Word Bank

animal trainer	doctor	firefighter	mayor	salesperson
city worker	factory	lawyer	minister	teacher
cleaner	worker	realtor	pharmacist	veterinarian
dentist	farmer	librarian	police officer	

51394—180 Days of Social Studies

© Shell Education

Name:_____ **Date:**_____

Directions: Look at the pictures, and read the text. Answer the questions.

A long time ago, Henry Ford liked to build machines and take them apart. He liked to invent, too.

Back then, cars cost too much money. Only rich people could afford them. Ford wanted to build a car for everyone. It would be a family car.

Ford invented the assembly line to build his cars. It moved car parts along a line. Workers added a part at each stop. Each car looked the same. The line could make many cars for less money. Ford called his car the Model T.

1. What did Henry Ford like to do?
   a. He liked to build houses.   c. He liked to build boats.
   b. He liked to build forts.   d. He liked to build machines.

2. What did Ford build?
   a. He built a big black box.   c. He built the Model F car.
   b. He built the Model T car.   d. He built a television set.

3. What did the assembly line do?
   a. build many cars for less money
   b. build few cars for lots of money
   c. build few cars for less money
   d. build many cars for lots of money

History

Name:_____ Date:_____

Directions: Look at the picture, and read the text. Answer the questions.

Orville and Wilbur Wright liked to build things. They liked to invent. They studied birds in flight. They built kites. Then, they designed an airplane. Orville flew it first. He flew at Kitty Hawk, North Carolina, in 1903. There were good winds and sand for a soft landing. He flew for 12 seconds. It was the first successful flight!

Today, people fly all over the world. They travel fast. They send letters and packages by airmail. The Air Force uses airplanes to protect us.

1. What did the Wright Brothers like to do?

   a. build sailboats
   b. build birdhouses
   c. build sand castles
   d. build things that could fly

2. What did the Wright Brothers design?

   a. the first airplane
   b. the first airplane that flew
   c. the first kite that flew
   d. the first glider that flew

3. Why are airplanes important?

_____

_____

51394—180 Days of Social Studies

© Shell Education

Name: _____ **Date:** _____

Directions: Look at the pictures. Answer the questions.

1. What do you see in the pictures?
    a. cars from long ago
    b. motorcycles from long ago
    c. walkers from long ago
    d. bicycles from long ago

2. How are they different from those of today?

    _____

    _____

3. What do you think they might look like in the future?

Name: _____ **Date:** _____

Directions: Look at the pictures. Answer the questions.

History

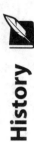

①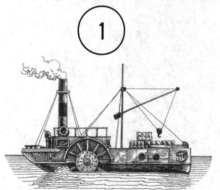

②

③

④

1. What order were these invented?

_____

_____

_____

_____

2. Would you like to take a ride in a boat? What kind? Why?

_____

_____

51394—180 Days of Social Studies

© Shell Education

Name: _____ **Date:** _____

Directions: Think about the inventions from long ago. Then, think about the inventions of today. Would you prefer to live then or now? Use words and pictures to tell why.

Inventions from Long Ago	Inventions of Today
I wish I could live long ago because…	I am happy to live now because…

Name: _____ Date: _____

Directions: Look at the picture, and read the text. Answer the questions.

We live in a democracy. Each person has a voice. Each person can vote for leaders. Our government is run by the people. It looks after the will of the people.

Our democracy is *representative*. This means we vote for leaders. They run our government for us. It is their job to look after the people. They make sure our rights are protected.

1. What is a democracy?

   a. People have a king.
   b. People have no say in their government.
   c. People vote for leaders, who work for them.
   d. People follow what the queen says.

2. What does *representative* mean?

   a. We are not represented.
   b. We are responsible for our own laws.
   c. A king or queen will look after the people.
   d. We vote for leaders who look after the people.

3. Based on the text, how do our government leaders look after the people?

   a. by ignoring people's rights
   b by protecting people's rights
   c. by looking out for themselves
   d. by doing very little

51394—180 Days of Social Studies
© Shell Education

Name: _____ **Date:** _____

Directions: Look at the diagram, and read the text. Answer the questions.

> We live in a democracy. These are the things we believe. We value the people. These are our values.

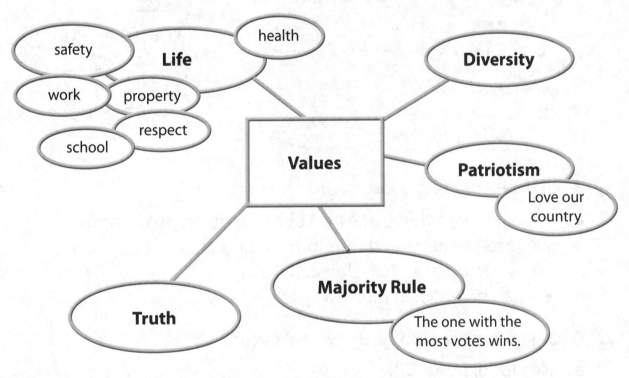

1. Which value shows we can be safe?

   a. truth   **c.** majority rule
   b. life   **d.** patriotism

2. Which value shows that we love our country?

   a. diversity   **c.** patriotism
   b. life   **d.** majority rule

3. Which value shows that the leader with the most votes wins?

   a. truth   **c.** majority rule
   b. life   **d.** patriotism

Civics

Name:_____ **Date:**_____

Directions: Look at the diagram. Answer the questions.

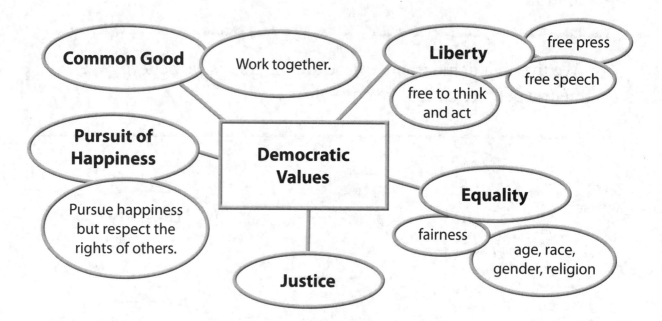

1. What does *common good* mean?

   a. We are free to think, act, and behave the way we want.
   b. We respect rights and freedoms of others.
   c. We work together to help each other.
   d. We can be equal in many ways.

2. What kinds are freedoms do we believe in?

   a. free food, free work
   b. free votes, free justice
   c. free speech, free press
   d. free politics, money, law

3. What does it mean to treat a person fairly and with equality?

   _____

   _____

   _____

51394—180 Days of Social Studies
© Shell Education

Name: _____ **Date:** _____

Directions: Read the text. Answer the questions.

Our Democratic Values	
common good	majority rule
life	liberty
pursuit of happiness	diversity
truth	equality
justice	patriotism

1. Which of the values says that we like how we are all different?

   a. justice
   b. diversity
   c. pursuit of happiness
   d. patriotism

2. Tell about one way you can show the value of truth.

   _____

   _____

3. Tell about one way you can work with others for the common good.

   _____

   _____

143

Civics

Name: _____ **Date:** _____

Directions: Read the text. Fill in the blanks with the missing values. Use the Word Bank to help you.

Value	What It Means	
	Pursue happiness but respect the rights of others.	
	People do not lie.	
	Love your country.	
	Work with other people to help everyone.	
	Treat all people in the same way.	
	You are free to speak and write what you think.	
	The leader with the most votes wins.	

Word Bank

common good	equality	patriotism
democracy	pursuit of happiness	truth
	liberty	

51394—180 Days of Social Studies

© Shell Education

Name:_____ **Date:**_____

Directions: Look at the picture, and read the text. Answer the questions.

People change the land. They cut down trees in forests. Farmers cut trees to plant crops. Some people cut trees to build houses and buildings.

Trees are important. They help clean the air. They give us shade. Tree roots hold the earth in place when it rains. We make things with wood from trees. We make furniture and build houses. But trees take a long time to grow again. We must protect our trees and forests.

1. Why do people cut down trees?

   a. They eat trees for food.

   b. They make plastic with them.

   c. They build houses with them.

   d. They make computers with them.

2. Why are trees important?

   a. because their leaves fall each year

   b. because they are green in the summer

   c. because they clean the air and give shade

   d. because squirrels like them

Name: _____ **Date:** _____

Directions: Look at the pictures, and read the text. Answer the questions.

Geography

People change the land. They build roads so we can get places. There are trails for walking. There are rails for trains. There are streets in towns and cities. There are small roads. And there are big superhighways. People pave over the land. Roads go through tunnels in the mountains. They cross bridges over water.

1. Towns and cities can be near water. What can we build to get over the water?

   a. tunnels   **c.** trails
   b. houses   **d.** bridges

2. Which one is *not* true?

   a. There are trails for trains.
   b. There are streets in towns.
   c. There are tunnels in mountains.
   d. There are roads and highways.

3. What are some places we can go when we follow roads? Think of places that are close and places that are far.

   _____

   _____

51394—180 Days of Social Studies   © Shell Education

Name: _____ **Date:** _____

Directions: Look at the picture, and answer the questions.

1. What did people do to change these waterways?

   a. They built a school.
   b. They built skyscrapers.
   c. They built a water canal.
   d. They built a park.

2. Look at the big ship. How will it move to higher water?

   a. A crane will move it up.
   b. It will take a road up.
   c. A bridge will move it up.
   d. A lock will move water up.

3. What waterway is close to where you live? Has it been changed by people? Tell how.

_____

_____

Geography

Name:_____ **Date:**_____

Directions: Look at the picture, and read the text. Answer the questions.

People change the land. They change the water and the air, too. They throw many things away. We throw wrappers and plastic bags away. We throw things that are broken away. We make lots of garbage. The garbage goes to landfills. There are many landfills in our country.

Some people throw garbage in the water. Cars and factories pollute the air. The land, the water, and the air become dirty. This is not a good change. We need to make our country a better place. We need to clean up. We need to recycle or reuse things.

1. What happens when we throw things away?
   a. They disappear.
   b. They go to another planet.
   c. They go to a landfill.
   d. They go to space.

2. What do we need to do to make our country a better place?
   a. make more landfills
   b. clean up and recycle
   c. throw garbage in the water
   d. drive more cars

3. How can you make the land, the water, and the air better?

_____

_____

51394—180 Days of Social Studies © Shell Education

Name:_____ **Date:**_____

Directions: Look at this picture. Answer the questions.

1. How is land that people change the same as the natural land? How is it different from the natural land?

_____

_____

_____

2. Draw a picture of what this land may have looked like before people changed it.

Economics

Name: _____ **Date:** _____

Directions: Read the text, and answer the questions.

> Producers make and sell goods and services. Making things costs them money.
>
> - They have to pay the people who work for them. They may be farmers or factory workers. They may sell things in a store. This is called *human resources*.
>
> - They have to pay for the things they use to make the goods. They may use wood, water, grain, or farm animals. These are called *natural resources*.
>
> - They have to pay for buildings and machines. They need trucks or cargo boxes to move the goods. They need money. These things are called *capital resources*.

1. What do producers need to pay for? Circle the three answers that are correct.

   a. capital resources   **c.** human resources
   b. natural resources   **d.** city resources

2. What are human resources?

   a. the cost of wood, water, and electricity
   b. the cost of people who work for the producer
   c. the cost of buildings, machines, and trucks
   d. the cost of people who buy the goods

3. What are capital resources?

   a. the cost of farmers who work for the producer
   b. the cost of wood, water, grain, or farm animals
   c. the cost of buildings, trucks, and machines
   d. the cost of factory workers who work for the producer

150

Name: _____ **Date:** _____

Directions: Look at the pictures, and read the text. Answer the questions.

Economics

How do producers pay for the resources? When they sell the goods and services, they make money. The money they make pays for the human resources. It also pays for the natural resources and the capital resources.

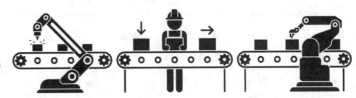

The goods they sell also need to make a profit. A *profit* is extra money. It is what is left when all resources have been paid for.

The cost and profit help the producer set the price for the goods. If the goods are scarce, then the producer can set a higher price.

1. How do producers make money?

   a. They sell their factory machines.
   b. They sell their capital resources.
   c. They sell their goods and services.
   d. They sell their profits.

2. What can the producer do if the goods are scarce?

   a. set the table   c. sell the factory
   b. set a higher price   d. sell the machines

Economics

Name:_____ **Date:**_____

Directions: Look at the pictures, and read the text. Answer the questions.

Costs are something you pay or lose. *Benefits* are something you get.

Cilla's lemonade stand is a wooden box. She made her best lemonade. She used fresh lemons, sugar, and mint.

Dee and Lars made a big, fancy stand. They added a roof. They made lemonade with a mix. They just added water.

1. What decisions did Cilla make when she made the lemonade?
   a. She used old lemons and water.
   b. She used a package mix and mint.
   c. She used a package mix and added water.
   d. She used fresh lemons, sugar, and mint.

2. Who made lemonade that cost more? Who made a stand that cost more?

   _____

   _____

3. Which lemonade do you think will sell best? Who will get the best benefit?

   _____

   _____

     © Shell Education

Name:_____ **Date:**_____

Directions: Look at the picture, and read the text. Answer the questions.

Here are Bev and Jen. They are having a yard sale. They are selling the toys they do not play with. They will buy new toys with the money they make.

1. What advice can you give Bev and Jen for displaying the toys?

   a. Hide the toys in a box.
   b. Spread the toys out on a table.
   c. Leave all the toys in your room.
   d. Put all the toys away.

2. How can Bev and Jen keep costs down? What decisions will help them sell more toys and get more benefits?

   _____

   _____

3. You want to make some money. What will you sell? Old toys? Something else? Tell about how you can set up a sale to get good benefits.

   _____

   _____

Economics

Name: _____ **Date:** _____

Directions: Read the table. Answer the question.

Rumpelstiltskin wants to spin some golden yarn. Help him make good decisions to keep costs low. Help him make a product that will sell well.

Work from home.	Pay money to buy a store.	Use real gold ($10).
Use some gold that is mixed with silver ($5).	Buy a brand new spinning wheel.	Buy a used spinning wheel. It works well.
Buy new clothes.	Wear his old clothes to work.	Rent a delivery truck.
Use his own van.	Sell the yarn.	Weave the yarn. Make nice scarves to sell.

1. Circle the good choices. Why are they good choices?

_____

_____

_____

_____

51394—180 Days of Social Studies

© Shell Education

Name:_____ Date:_____

Directions: Look at the pictures, and read the text. Answer the questions.

Television Long Ago, 1950	Television Now

• **fuzzy pictures** • **black, white, and gray** • **sound not clear** • **controls on the television** • **all about the same size** • **screen was rounded** • **needed time to warm up** • **a few channels** • **some TV shows**	• **clear pictures** • **color** • **sharp sound** • **remote control** • **sizes: small, medium, large, very large** • **screen is flat** • **turns on right away** • **many channels** • **many TV shows**

1. What were TV pictures like long ago?

   a. clear   **c.** fuzzy

   b. color   **d.** like the ones today

2. How do you turn on a TV today? How did you turn on a TV long ago?

   _____

3. Would you like to watch a TV from long ago or one from today? Why?

   _____

   _____

History

Name: _____ Date: _____

Directions: Look at the pictures, and read the text. Answer the questions.

These telephones have wires. They connect to a wall.		
1. crank telephone	2. dial telephone	3. push-button telephone

These phones have no wires. You can walk around with them.		
4. cordless phone	5. mobile phone	6. cell phone

1. How were old telephones different?

   a. They had screens.
   b. They had no wires.
   c. They had headsets.
   d. They had wires.

2. What do new phones have that old ones did not?

   a. They all have wires.
   b. They all have buttons.
   c. They all have screens.
   d. They all have wood.

3. Why is it better to have a phone with no wires?

   a. It costs less money.
   b. You can walk around with it.
   c. It costs more money.
   d. You can swim with it.

 © Shell Education

History

Name: _____ **Date:** _____

Directions: Look at the pictures, and read the text. Answer the questions.

The first computers were big. They worked with codes and numbers.

Computers today are small. They do many things.

1. What were the first computers like?

   a. They were much smaller.   **c.** They were laptops.
   b. They were like tablets.   **d.** They were very big.

2. Computers of today are different. How?

   a. They only work with codes and numbers.
   b. They are smaller. You can do many things.
   c. They are bigger. You cannot do many things.
   d. They are bigger. They only work with numbers.

3. What things can you do on a computer?

   _____

   _____

History

Name: _____ **Date:** _____

Directions: Look at the time line. Read the text, and answer the questions.

Cameras are like little machines. The pictures help you remember. You can remember your family. You can remember your friends. You can remember your party. You can remember many things.

Long Ago	Then	Next	Later	Now
This one looked like a box. It was big and heavy. It was hard to use. You put film in it.	This one had a flashbulb. You put film in it. Then, the film went to a lab to make pictures.	The picture came out of this camera. You put picture film in it.	You can throw this camera away.	This one is on a cell phone.

1. What did people put in cameras long ago?

   a. pictures   c. film
   b. paper   d. water

2. What camera do you use? Why do you take pictures?

   _____

   _____

   _____

Name:_____ **Date:**_____

Directions: Think about the inventions from long ago. Then, think about how they have changed. What is one thing that makes each invention better today?

Inventions from Long Ago	Inventions of Today
1. television 	
2. telephone 	
3. computer 	
4. camera 	

Civics

Name:_____ Date:_____

Directions: Look at the picture, and read the text. Answer the questions.

It takes a lot of money to run the government. The government needs money for many things. It pays workers. It gives services to people. It fixes things in the town or city.

Where does the government get money? Citizens pay taxes. Tax money goes to the government. Adults pay taxes. You may pay taxes, too.

1. What are taxes?

   a. food
   b. transportation
   c. money
   d. government

2. Why does the government need tax money?

   a. Taxes pay for our cars.
   b. Taxes pay for our toys.
   c. Taxes pay for our volunteers.
   d. Taxes pay for services.

3. Which one is *not* true?

   a. Adults pay taxes.
   b. You may pay taxes.
   c. Citizens pay taxes.
   d. People don't pay taxes.

© Shell Education

Name: _____ **Date:** _____

Directions: Look at the pictures, and read the text. Answer the questions.

 **Property Tax**	When you own a house, you pay taxes. When you own land, you pay taxes. Every year, you need to pay money to the government.
 **Sales Tax**	When you buy something at a store, you pay taxes. If you buy a toy, you pay sales tax. When your family buys a car, you pay sales tax. In some states, there is no sales tax on some things, such as food in a grocery store.
 **Income Tax**	People who work at jobs pay income tax. When they make more money, they pay more taxes.

1. What is the tax on houses and land?

   a. sales tax
   b. income tax
   c. property tax
   d. medical tax

2. On which items do you pay sales tax?

   a. on the money you make at work
   b. on your house or land
   c. on land that you own
   d. on toys, laptops, and cars

3. What happens to people who make more money at their jobs?

_____

Civics

Name: _____ **Date:** _____

Directions: Look at the diagram. Answer the questions.

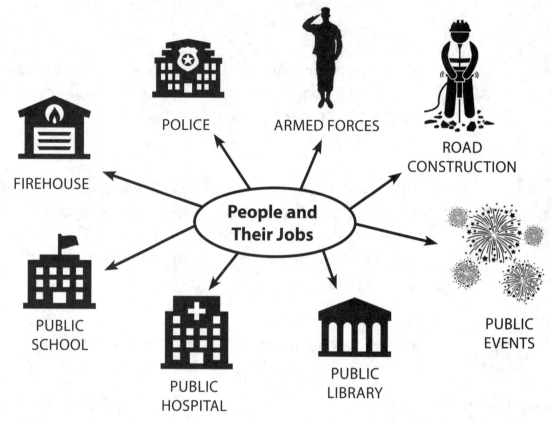

1. What could you see on the Fourth of July that is paid by taxes?
   a. hot dogs
   b. cotton candy
   c. ice cream
   d. fireworks

2. Think about your community. Who is paid by taxes?

   _____

   _____

   _____

   _____

© Shell Education

Name: _____ **Date:** _____

Directions: Look at the diagram. Answer the questions.

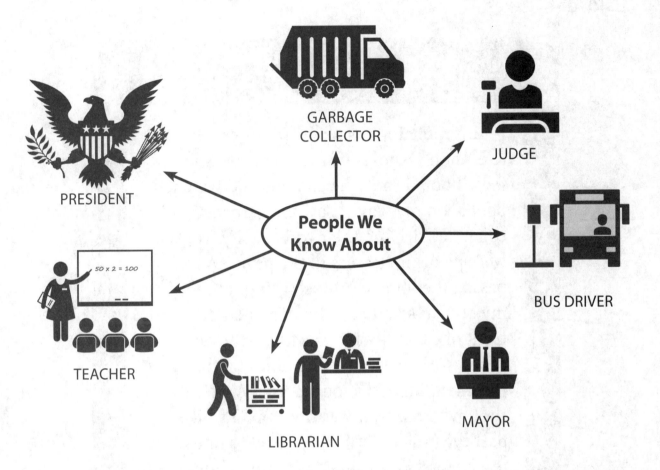

GARBAGE
COLLECTOR

JUDGE

PRESIDENT

People We
Know About

BUS DRIVER

50 x 2 = 100

TEACHER

LIBRARIAN

MAYOR

1. Which of these people help you learn to read?

   a. president and mayor
   b. librarian and teacher
   c. judge and garbage collector
   d. mayor and judge

2. Tell about the people who keep your town clean. Are they paid by taxes?

   _____

   _____

   _____

Civics

Name: _____ **Date:** _____

Directions: List some of the things mentioned in the text that are paid for by taxes.

> This morning, I saw the president on television. After I ate my breakfast, I left for school. I took the city bus and watched people on my way. I saw the garbage collectors driving their truck. City workers were planting flowers in the park. We passed the library. Oops! I forgot to bring my book back. I saw the mayor standing in front of city hall. He was talking to a judge. More workers were fixing holes in the street. Just then, I heard a loud noise. A fire truck shot by! Finally, it was my stop. I walked past the police station. I waved to one of the teachers when I walked into the school yard.

_____

_____

_____

_____

          © Shell Education

Name: _____   **Date:** _____

Directions: Look at the picture, and read the text. Answer the questions.

> We are consumers. We buy and use many things. We get many things from nature. We get gas and oil from nature. Gas and oil are under the ground. We drill in the ground and work on rigs. We pump the oil up from way down in the ground. There is oil in some states, such as Texas, California, Oklahoma, and Louisiana.
>
> We need oil and gas to run our cars and trucks. Oil and gas heat our houses and buildings. We use oil to make other things, such as plastic, clothing, and paint. Oil is also used to make tar for roads and roofs.

1. What does *consumer* mean?

   a. a person who builds a lot of things
   b. a person who sells a lot of things
   c. a person who buys, gets, and uses things
   d. a person who makes things to sell

2. Based on the text, which states have oil?

   a. Texas, Florida, Georgia, and Vermont
   b. Texas, California, Oklahoma, and Louisiana
   c. Texas, California, Oregon, and Michigan
   d. Texas, New York, North Carolina, and Nevada

3. Which one is *not* true?

   a. We use oil to heat our houses and make things.
   b. We use oil to run our cars and trucks.
   c. We use oil and gas to make things, such as plastic.
   d. We use oil and gas on our food.

Name: _____   Date: _____

Directions: Look at the pictures, and read the text. Answer the questions.

Geography

We take many things from the earth. Miners mine sand and gravel to build roads. They look for minerals and metals in the ground. Diamonds, gold, and silver are used to make fine rings and things. Copper is used to make wire.

Some mines are open. They look like big holes in the ground. Some mines are closed. The miners work underground. This can be dangerous. They use an elevator and walk through underground tunnels. Miners drive big trucks and use special machines.

1. What are some things that people mine from the earth?

   a. wood and pulp

   b. cotton and wool

   c. food, such as apples

   d. diamonds and gold

2. How can we use copper?

   a. make paper with it

   b. make wire with it

   c. make plastic with it

   d. make soap with it

3. Why do you think mining underground is dangerous?

   _____

51394—180 Days of Social Studies   © Shell Education

Name: _____ **Date:** _____

Directions: Look at the map, and read the text. Answer the questions.

    Some fishers work on factory ships. They freeze fish on the boat. Most fishers work in gulfs and oceans. Many people like to eat fish.

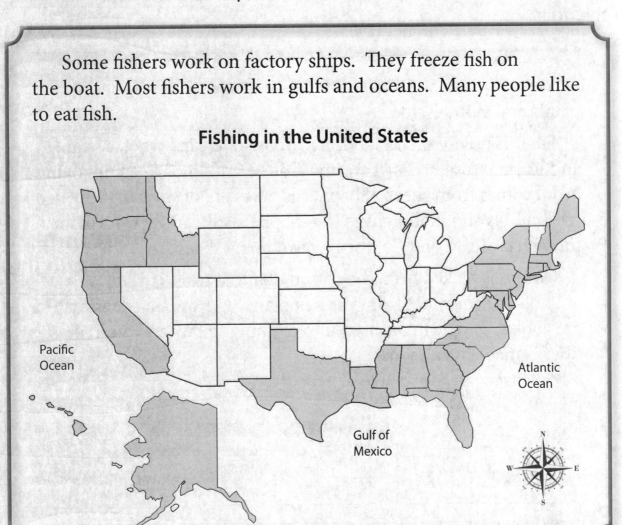

Fishing in the United States

Pacific Ocean

Atlantic Ocean

Gulf of Mexico

1. Based on the map, where do most fishers fish?

    a. in the gulf and oceans
    b. in the lakes and creeks
    c. in the creeks and rivers
    d. in the falls and rivers

2. Why is it important to catch lots of different fish?

_____

_____

Geography

Name:_____ **Date:**_____

Directions: Look at the pictures, and read the text. Answer the questions.

> We grow plants and raise animals for food. Fiber comes from plants and animals, too.
>
> Fiber is used to make clothing. Some fibers are wool, cotton, and linen. Wool keeps us warm. Cotton and linen keep us cool. Wool comes from sheep. Shepherds take care of sheep. Sheep can live on hills and mountains. The shepherds shear the wool from the sheep. Texas and California have many sheep.
>
> Cotton is picked from the cotton plant. It grows in states that are hot. Linen comes from the flax plant. It grows in states that are cooler. People make fiber into clothing to buy and wear. Some fiber is made by humans.
>
>

1. Why do farmers grow plants and raise animals?

   a. to keep them as pets
   b. for food and clothing
   c. for lighting our homes
   d. to make electricity

2. When can you wear wool? When can you wear cotton or linen clothes?

   _____

   _____

Name: _____ **Date:** _____

Directions: Read the text, and complete the chart.

> Our country is rich in many ways. We have products from oil and gas, mines, fishing, and fiber. Describe things we make or get from each one.

Oil and Gas 	
Mines 	
Fishing 	
Fiber 	

Economics

Name:_____ Date:_____

Directions: Look at the picture, and read the text. Answer the questions.

You know how to make money. You can start a small business, such as selling lemonade. You can save your allowance. You can sell old toys you do not use anymore.

Where do you keep your money? You can put it in your piggy bank at home. This is a good idea if you have a little bit of money. If you have a lot of money, there is a better place to keep it safe. It is a bank!

Banks keep your money safe so no one can steal it. When you keep your money in the bank, you will make some more money. This money is called *interest*.

1. Where is a good place to keep a small amount of money?

   a. in a hole
   b. in a shed
   c. in a piggy bank
   d. in the fish tank

2. What is a safe place to keep a lot of money?

   a. in a piggy bank
   b. in a word bank
   c. in a river bank
   d. in a bank

3. What is interest?

   a. It is a place for your piggy bank.
   b. It is the money the bank pays you.
   c. It is a hiding place.
   d. It is a safe place.

51394—180 Days of Social Studies

© Shell Education

Name: _____ **Date:** _____

Directions: Look at the picture, and read the text. Answer the questions.

Economics

Why put your money in a bank? If you keep your money in your pocket, you may want to spend it. It may get lost or stolen. If you keep your money in a piggy bank, it is easy to get to and spend.

If you want to save your money, keep it in a savings account at the bank. If your money is not close by, it will be harder to spend. It will be easier to save. The money will be safe.

If the bank is not open, you can use an ATM. Your parents can show you how. It is a machine. You can put money in or take money out of your account. You will need a bank card and a password.

1. What is a good place to keep your money if you want to save it?
   a. in your pocket
   b. in your piggy bank
   c. in a savings account
   d. in the barn

2. The bank is closed. You want to take money out of your account. What can you do?
   a. Use your bank card at the ATM.
   b. Use your library card at the ATM.
   c. Get upset.
   d. Never go to the bank again.

Economics

Name: _____ **Date:** _____

Directions: Look at the pictures, and read the text. Answer the questions.

Saving for a Short Time	Saving for a Long Time
These do not cost very much. 	These cost more money. 

1. Look at the chart. Place an **X** on each item that is in the wrong box.

2. What would you like to save for? Will you save for a short time or a long time?

   _____

   _____

   _____

3. Which one can you buy after saving for only a short while?

   a. computer   **c.** video game console
   b. cell phone   **d.** teddy bear

  © Shell Education

Name: _____ **Date:** _____

Directions: Look at the pictures, and read the text. Answer the questions.

Economics

The bank tracks your money. It records how much money you save. It notes how much interest you make. This is printed in your passbook.

Here is Henry's passbook. He deposits his allowance each week.

Here is your passbook. You want to save your allowance each week.

Date	Deposit
March 10	$10
March 17	$10
March 24	$10
March 31	$10
March 31: interest	$1
April 7	$10
April 14	$10

Date	Deposit

1. Your allowance is $5 each week. Fill in the passbook to show how much money you will deposit.

2. How will you use a passbook?
   a. to read a story from it   c. to track your money
   b. to learn math in it   d. to draw in it

3. Look at Henry's passbook. How often do you think the bank gives him interest?

_____

© Shell Education

Economics

Name: _____ **Date:** _____

Directions: Read the journal. Choose the correct word for each blank from the Word Bank. Write it on the line.

Mom said I had too much money for my piggy

_____. Today, I went to the bank with Mom. I

opened a savings _____. The teller was very

nice. She gave me a _____ to track

my money. She said that at the end of the month, I will

get _____ on my money. That makes

me happy. I am saving for a laptop. I will save for a

_____ time. It costs a lot of money! The teller said

not to worry if I want to deposit money and the bank

is closed. I can use the _____ . She showed

me how to use it. I even have a bank _____ to put

in the machine. I will make sure to remember my

_____.

Word Bank

| account | card | long | password |
| bank | interest | passbook | ATM |

 © Shell Education

Name: _____ **Date:** _____

Directions: Look at the picture, and read the text. Answer the questions.

A community is a group of people. They live in the same area. It might be a neighborhood. It might be a town. The people work there, too. They help each other.

Here is a picture of a community long ago. It was not very big. It was a new community. Later, more people came. Then, the town grew.

Why did the town grow? This place needed a doctor. It needed a storekeeper. It needed a teacher. It needed a cooper, too. It needed many workers. These people came to the town. Then, the town grew. Communities like this changed over time.

1. **What is a community?**

   a. It is a group of animals.   **c.** It is a group of toys.
   b. It is a group of people.   **d.** It is a group of stores.

2. **Why did the community grow?**

   a. It needed many horses.   **c.** It needed many workers.
   b. It needed many tools.   **d.** It needed many foods.

3. **What happens to communities over time? Circle all the correct answers.**

   a. They stay exactly the same.
   b. They change in some way.
   c. They have new people come to stay.
   d. They grow in size.

History

Name: _____ **Date:** _____

Directions: Look at the pictures, and read the text. Answer the questions.

Here are houses from long ago.

These houses were made of wood. There were many trees. The workers cut the trees into boards. They built the houses with the boards.

These houses were made of bricks. They also have wood. Brick houses were very solid.

Here are houses of today.

This house is made of many things. There are bricks. There is metal. There is plastic, too. There is a garage for a car.

This is an apartment building. It is made of many materials. There is steel and glass.

---

1. What were the houses made of long ago?

   a. steel and concrete   **c.** plastic and bricks
   b. steel and plastic   **d.** wood and bricks

2. What is different about the houses today?

   _____

   _____

   _____

Name: _____ Date: _____

Directions: Look at the pictures, and read the text. Answer the questions.

Long ago, people walked in their communities.

Today, people travel together. They can take a bus or a subway train.

People can travel alone. They can go anywhere. People can take a taxi or a car.

1. Which one is correct?
    a. Long ago, people might take a taxi.
    b. Long ago, people might take a bus.
    c. Long ago, people might take a subway train.
    d. Long ago, people walked a lot.

2. What are some ways people travel in their communities today?

   _____

3. How do you travel in your community?

   _____

History

Name:_____ **Date:**_____

Directions: Look at the picture, and read the text. Answer the questions.

Long ago, people traveled by walking. Sometimes, they would ride horses. Or, they might ride in carts, wagons, or coaches.

Travel has changed. Roads have changed, too. Long ago, roads were made of earth. When it rained, the roads turned to mud. They might have holes. It was hard to travel. Sometimes, roads were made of cobblestone. They were very bumpy.

Today, many roads are made of asphalt. They are smooth to drive on. They are wide across. They are made for cars, trucks, and bicycles.

1. How did people travel long ago?

   a. They rode in buses.
   b. They rode in cars and trucks.
   c. They rode in subway trains.
   d. They rode in carts or coaches.

2. What happened to earth roads when it rained?

   a. They turned to stone.
   b. They turned to mud.
   c. Nothing happened to the roads.
   d. They were easy to travel.

3. What are the roads like in your community?

_____

Name: _____ **Date:** _____

Directions: Compare your community today to life in a community long ago. What is the same? What is different? Complete the Venn diagram.

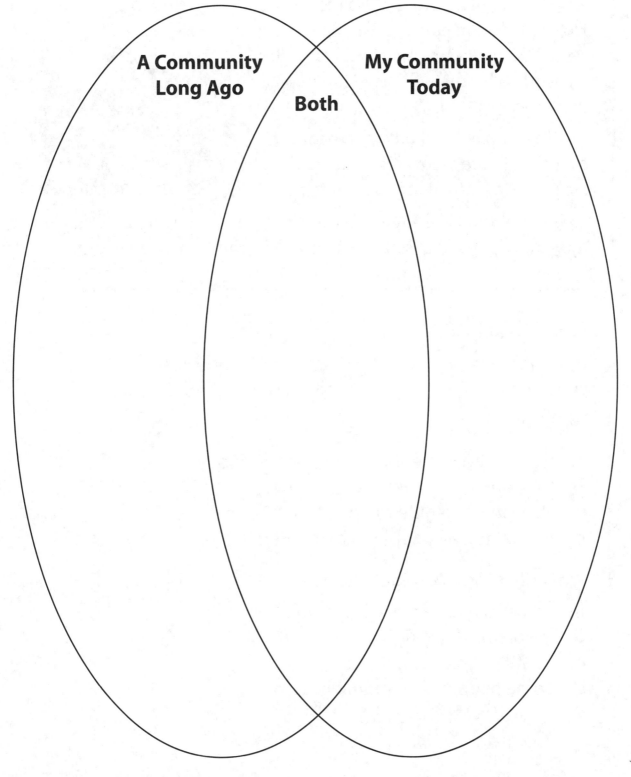

A Community Long Ago

Both

My Community Today

Civics

Name:_____ **Date:**_____

Directions: Look at the picture, and read the text. Answer the questions.

> Martin Luther King Jr. was a minister. He wanted all people to have the same civil rights. King became a civil rights leader. He worked hard for all people to be treated the same.
>
>
>
> King traveled and talked to people all over the United States. He led marches. He protested laws that were not fair.
>
> In 1964, the Civil Rights Act was passed. It said all people have the same rights. It passed because of King and others like him.

1. Who was King?

   a. a librarian   **c.** a civil rights leader

   b. a senator   **d.** a high school teacher

2. What did King want?

   a. He wanted all people to be treated poorly.

   b. He wanted to travel and have fun.

   c. He wanted people to not be treated the same.

   d. He wanted all people to be treated the same.

3. What does the Civil Rights Act say?

   a. All people have the same rights.

   b. No people have rights.

   c. Some people have rights.

   d. Some people have more rights.

51394—180 Days of Social Studies

© Shell Education

Name: _____ **Date:** _____

Directions: Look at the picture, and read the text. Answer the questions.

Amelia Earhart wanted to fly. She worked hard to save money. She bought a plane. She learned to fly and became a pilot. It was a long time ago when women did not fly planes.

Earhart flew across the Atlantic Ocean. It took 14 hours. The weather was very bad. She was the first female pilot to do this alone.

Earhart set many records for flying. She wrote books about her flights. She stood for equal rights for men and women. She showed courage. She believed in equality.

1. What did Earhart want to become?

   a. a school teacher   **c.** a farmer
   b. a dentist   **d.** a pilot

2. Which one is *not* true?

   a. Earhart bought a plane.
   b. A long time ago women did not fly planes.
   c. She wanted to drive on a safari in Africa.
   d. She set many records for flying.

3. How did Earhart show good citizenship?

   _____

   _____

Civics

Name: _____ **Date:** _____

Directions: Look at the pictures, and read the text. Answer the questions.

	Who	They Showed...
Helen Keller	• deaf and blind • worked for people's rights	• courage • respect
Theodore Roosevelt	• youngest president	• courage • fairness
Sojourner Truth	• helped African Americans • worked for their rights	• courage • equality • truth
George Washington	• first president	• courage • honesty

1. What is one thing that is the same for all four people?

   a. justice   **c.** humor
   b. courage   **d.** equality

2. Who were the presidents?

   a. Keller and Truth   **c.** Washington and Keller
   b. Truth and Washington **d.** Roosevelt and Washington

3. Who do you think worked to help other people?

_____

51394—180 Days of Social Studies

© Shell Education

Name: _____ **Date:** _____

Directions: Look at the picture, and read the text. Answer the questions.

The Navajo people are American Indians. The Code Talkers were Marines. They helped during wars. They used the Navajo language to make up a code. They learned the code when they were training. They had to remember the code. They did not take the code book to war so the enemy could not get it.

The Code Talkers kept soldiers safe. They sent secret messages. They called for more guns. They moved soldiers. They saved lives. The enemy did not know what the Code Talkers were saying.

Code Talkers statue in Arizona.

1. What did the Code Talkers do to help our soldiers?

   a. built a statue   **c.** liked to talk
   b. started a war   **d.** made up a code

2. Why were the Code Talkers good citizens?

   _____

   _____

3. How have you helped other people?

   _____

   _____

Civics

Name:_____ **Date:**_____

Directions: Look at the pictures. Answer the questions.

1. Who are these people? Circle the ones you know
   something about.

2. Why were they good citizens?

_____

_____

_____

_____

_____

© *Shell Education*

Name: _____ **Date:** _____

Directions: Read the text, and answer the questions.

Geography

> Long ago, settlers brought new ideas to our country. The people came from far away. Travel by boat was slow. Travel by walking or horse was slow, too. It took a long time for people to move from one place to another place. It took a long time to deliver mail. It took a long time for new ideas to be shared.
>
> Today, ideas move quickly. We talk on the phone to people far away. We send email to people everywhere. We send text messages. We see the news on television. We read what happened in newspapers. We shop and buy things from the Internet. Our phones, computers, and televisions move ideas very fast!

1. How did ideas move long ago?

    a. They moved quickly from one place to another.
    b. They did not move at all.
    c. They only moved by mail.
    d. They moved slowly from one place to another.

2. How do ideas move quickly today?

    a. by horse or walking
    b. by phone and computer
    c. by tractor
    d. by settlers long ago

3. How do we buy things today? Circle all correct answers.

    a. We shop by mail.
    b. We walk to a store.
    c. We buy on the Internet.
    d. We go by horse and cart.

Geography

Name: _____ **Date:** _____

Directions: Look at the pictures, and read the text. Answer the questions.

> We move things in many ways. We move some oil and gas with pipelines. We build pipelines across the land. Oil and gas are pumped through big steel pipes.
>
> We move food. Some food grows close to our home. Some food comes from far away, such as fruit from Mexico, nuts from Brazil, or meat from Canada. The food travels on trucks and trains. Special boxes keep food cool and fresh.
>
> We move things to factories. We move metals, plastic, and fiber. They go on trains, trucks, boats, and planes. We make products with them. Then, we move products to the stores. Then, people can buy them.

1. How do we move some oil and gas?

   a. We use cars.   **c.** We use pipelines.
   b. We use motorcycles.   **d.** We use horses.

2. How do we move food to stores?

   a. in special envelopes
   b. in boxes that stay cool
   c. in paper bags
   d. in shopping carts

3. Name some places where our food comes from. What kinds of food come from other countries?

_____

51394—180 Days of Social Studies   © Shell Education

Name:_____ **Date:**_____

Directions: Look at the pictures, and read the text. Answer the questions.

After Natural Disasters

after a tornado

after an earthquake

after a hurricane

1. What may happen to people, ideas, and goods if there is a natural disaster?

   a. They will keep moving like they always do.

   b. They will move with horses and wagons.

   c. They will move with difficulty or not at all.

   d. They will move with cars and buses.

2. What is your school or home plan for a natural disaster?

   _____

   _____

   _____

   _____

   _____

   _____

Geography

Name: _____ **Date:** _____

Directions: Look at the pictures, and read the text. Answer the questions.

Some people move where the weather is warm and rainy.	Some people move to a new city. They may go to a new school.	Some people move to a new country. They may come from war. They may come for work.

1. Why do some people move to a new country?

   a. They come to live in war.

   b. They come to live in factories.

   c. They come to do no work.

   d. They come to work.

2. Why do some people move to a new city or state?

   a. They go to a new school.

   b. They start a new job.

   c. They move where the weather is warm.

   d. all of the above

3. How do people move from one place to another?

   _____

   _____

   _____

51394—180 Days of Social Studies © Shell Education

Name:_____ **Date:**_____

Directions: People, ideas, and things move. Tell about how and why they move.

	How and Why They Move
People 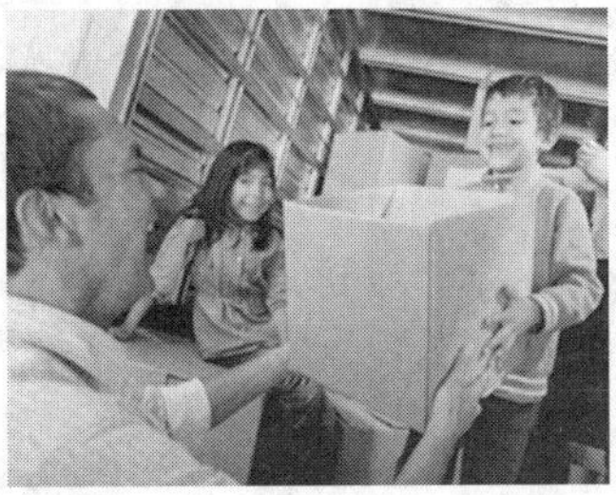	
Ideas 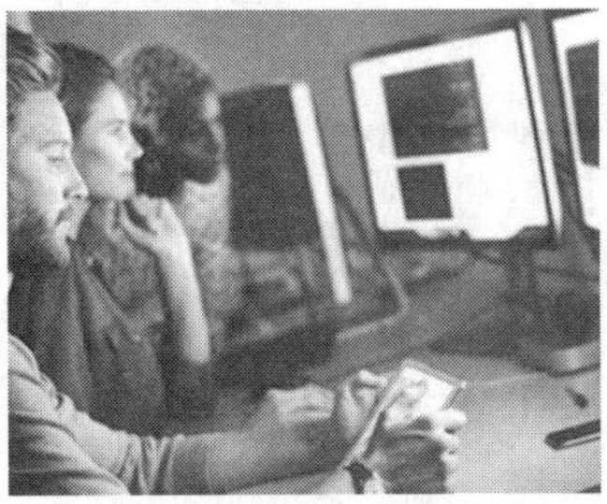	
Things 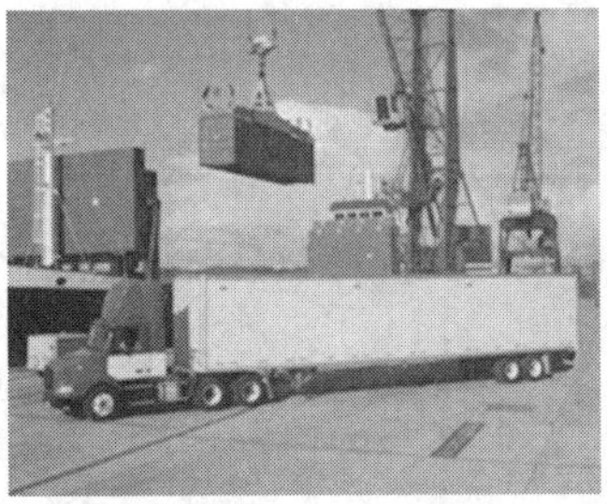	

Geography

Economics

Name: _____ **Date:** _____

Directions: Look at the picture, and read the text. Answer the questions.

Producers use natural resources to make things. Some natural resources come from the lakes and oceans. Some resources come from the trees and forests. We get resources from the earth, such as on farms. We get natural resources from under the earth. Oil, gas, and minerals come from under the earth.

Do you know where paper comes from? Where do we get what we need to make bread? Where does your T-shirt come from? All of these things come from natural resources that go into production. This changes the resources.

1. What are natural resources?

   a. things that come from a factory
   b. things that come from a school
   c. things that come from a store
   d. things that come from nature

2. Where do oil, gas, and minerals come from?

   a. the closet
   b. the kitchen
   c. underground
   d. the barn

3. What happens to natural resources that go into production?

   a. They get changed.
   b. They do not change at all.
   c. They go into hiding.
   d. They stay natural resources.

© Shell Education

Name:_____ **Date:**_____

Directions: Look at the pictures, and read the text. Answer the questions.

How do we change natural resources? Here are some products. They come from natural resources. Tell where they come from.

1. Where does bread come from?

   a. a vegetable   **c.** a grain
   b. a fruit   **d.** a meat

2. Where does a notebook come from?

   a. grain   **c.** fruit
   b. meat   **d.** trees

3. Where do yogurt and other dairy products come from?

   _____

   _____

   _____

Economics

Name: _____ **Date:** _____

Directions: Look at the chart, and answer the questions.

From Wheat to Bread

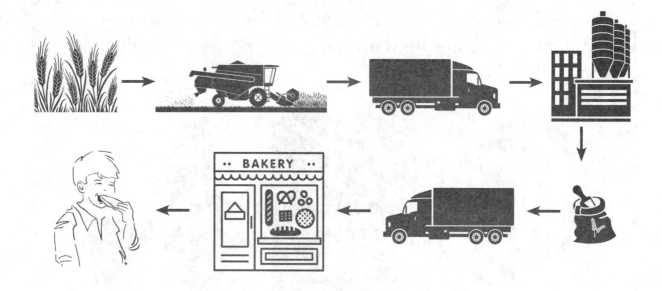

1. What does the factory turn the wheat grain into?

   a. glue   **c.** erasers

   b. flour   **d.** pencils

2. Put the steps in correct order.

Step Number	Step Description
	The wheat grows in the field.
	The flour travels to a bakery.
	The baker makes the bread.
	The wheat is milled. It becomes flour.
	The farmer harvests the wheat.
	The wheat travels to a factory.
	The baker sells the bread.
	The flour is put in bags.
	We buy and eat the bread.

© Shell Education

Name: _____ **Date:** _____

Directions: Look at the pictures, and read the text. Answer the questions.

Economics

Cotton grows in 17 states! It grows in the South. Would you like to know how your T-shirt or sweater is made?

The cotton is picked in the fields. People used to hand-pick cotton. Now they use machines. The machines bale the cotton. The bales are trucked to a factory. The cotton is washed. Then, machines spin the cotton into thread or yarn. Now, machines take the thread and weave it into cloth on looms. The cloth is used to make T-shirts and other clothing.

1. People used to pick cotton by hand. What is used now?

   a. shovels   **c.** machines
   b. rakes   **d.** hammers

2. Imagine you work in cotton production. Where will you work? Will you work in a field? Or will you work in a factory or in a store? Why?

   _____

3. Do you live in a cotton state? Or, would you like to visit a cotton state? Tell about what you would see in the fields.

   _____

   _____

Economics

Name:_____ Date:_____

Directions: Choose the correct phrase for each picture from the Word Bank.

Here is how tomato sauce is made. Label each step in the production.

_____

_____

_____

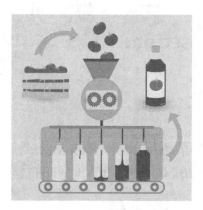

_____

_____

_____

Word Bank

factory: wash, crush, and make sauce   tomatoes in the field
sauce on the store shelves   transport to factory
tomato harvest   transport to store

© Shell Education

ANSWER KEY

Week 1—History

Day 1
1. b
2. d

Day 2
1. d
2. b
3. d

Day 3
1. b
2. d
3. Responses will vary.

Day 4
1. a
2. Responses will vary.
3. Responses will vary.

Day 5
1. Responses will vary but will relate to neighbor and/or community services.

Week 2—Civics

Day 1
1. b
2. c
3. d

Day 2
1. c
2. d
3. Responses will vary.

Day 3
1. b
2. c
3. Responses will vary.

Day 4
1. d
2. d
3. Responses will vary.

Day 5
1. Responses will vary but will relate to helping, caring, kindness, generosity, and so on.

Week 3—Geography

Day 1
1. a
2. Students will print letters on correct places on the map.
3. b

Day 2
1. b
2. c
3. d

Day 3
1. d
2. c
3. Responses will vary but may relate to playground equipment, other buildings or structures, and so on.

Day 4
1. Students will draw on the legend and map.
2. Responses will vary.

Day 5
1. east on Dock Street, north on Dickory Street, and east on Mouse Street

Week 4—Economics

Day 1
1. d
2. b
3. b

Day 2
1. c
2. c
3. c

Day 3
1. goods: pizza; teddy bear; shoe services: teaching; cutting hair; dental work
2. d
3. c

195

ANSWER KEY *(cont.)*

Day 4
1. c
2. It travels by truck, train, boat, or airplane.
3. It travels from the factory by truck, train, boat, or airplane. It is delivered to the store. I go to the store with (mom, dad, others). I buy the bear and take it home.

Day 5
1. The following are circled:
   goods: food; soccer ball; computer; cell phone
   services: the work of police officer, baker, shoe repair, cashier
   goods and services in your community: haircut; car repair; restaurant; toy shop/sales
   producers: bakery; farmer; factory
   distribution: truck; train; airplane; ship

Week 5—History

Day 1
1. b
2. c
3. d

Day 2
1. a
2. d
3. c

Day 3
1. b
2. d
3. Responses will vary but may relate to learning to read, working hard, and/or learning about science.

Day 4
1. b
2. Responses will vary.

Day 5
1. Responses will vary.
2. Responses will vary.

Week 6—Civics

Day 1
1. b
2. c

Day 2
1. b
2. c
3. Responses will vary but may relate to freedom, justice, and so on.

Day 3
1. d
2. c
3. Responses will vary but will relate to freedom.

Day 4
1. b
2. c
3. Responses will vary but may relate to strength, freedom, leadership, and so on.

Day 5
1. Responses will vary but will relate to the following:
   Our Flag: justice; bravery; purity; freedom; and so on.
   The Statue of Liberty: liberty; freedom
   The Great Seal: strength; beauty; freedom, long life; protection; peace; glory; standing together

Week 7—Geography

Day 1
1. c
2. Responses will be added to map.
3. d

Day 2
1. b
2. a
3. Response will be added to map.

Day 3
1. c
2. a
3. Responses will be added to map.

51394—180 Days of Social Studies

© Shell Education

ANSWER KEY *(cont.)*

Day 4
1. Responses will be added to compass rose.
2. Responses will vary.

Day 5
1–4. Responses will be added to map.

Week 8—Economics

Day 1
1. c
2. d
3. b

Day 2
1. b
2. d
3. c

Day 3
1. c
2. b
3. It will take 3 weeks. She will save $10 each week. $10 + $10 + $10 = $30

Day 4
1. d
2. $5 each week
3. Add more money to the "Saving" column and have less money in the "Spending" column.

Day 5
1. Responses will vary.

Week 9—History

Day 1
1. a
2. b
3. c

Day 2
1. a
2. a

Day 3
1. d
2. b
3. Responses will vary but will relate to uses for peanuts for food and products.

Day 4
1. Today, many African Americans play baseball.
2. Responses will vary but may relate to bravery, persistence, and so on.

Day 5
1. Responses will vary but may relate to: same: firsts; brave; leaders; caring different: backgrounds/cultures; leader/inventor/baseball player

Week 10—Civics

Day 1
1. d
2. c
3. b

Day 2
1. b
2. d
3. Responses will vary but may relate to love and beauty.

Day 3
1. c
2. d
3. Responses will vary but may relate to the Statue of Liberty, the flag, and so on.

Day 4
1. b
2. c
3. Responses will vary.

Day 5
1. Responses will vary.

© Shell Education

ANSWER KEY *(cont.)*

Week 11—Geography

Day 1
1. Responses will be added to map.
2. b
3. a

Day 2
1. b
2. c
3. Africa, Antarctica, Australia, South America

Day 3
1. d
2. b
3. Three of the following: South America, Africa, Asia

Day 4
1. b
2. Responses will vary.

Day 5
Responses will be added to map.

Week 12—Economics

Day 1
1. a
2. d
3. b

Day 2
1. b
2. c
3. Responses will vary.

Day 3
1. b
2. d
3. Ellie will trade with Mr. Green. It is a better trade. She will get more in return.

Day 4
1. b
2. You will buy pants at Wilton Mall for $15. You will buy a puzzle at Belmont Mall for $6. These cost less.
3. Responses will vary.

Day 5
trade: Two people have goods. They change one for the other. They do not buy the goods with money.
consumers: They buy goods and services.
producers: They make and sell goods and services.
market: It is where producers sell and consumers buy.
competition: All the producers try to be the best. They want the consumer to buy their product.
goods: These are the things that we buy.
services: The actions or jobs that producers do.

Week 13—History

Day 1
1. b
2. c
3. d

Day 2
1. d
2. b

Day 3
1. d
2 a
3. Responses will vary but will relate to teaching, theories, or nuclear energy.

Day 4
1. b
2. Responses will vary.

Day 5
Responses will vary but may include:
Pasteur: scientist; pasteurization; vaccine
Meir: Israel; prime minister
Einstein: Theory; Relativity; nuclear energy
Bell: inventor; telephone (allow for metal detector; audiometer)

© Shell Education

ANSWER KEY *(cont.)*

Week 14—Civics

Day 1
1. c
2. b
3. d

Day 2
1. b
2. c
3. Cross the street at a crosswalk.

Day 3
1. a
2. c
3. Her sword stands for punishment. Those who do bad things will get punished.

Day 4
1. c
2. d
3. Responses will vary.

Day 5
R—We work quietly in class. L—We stop at a stop sign. L—We do not steal. R—We do not run in the hallway. L—We do not litter in the park. R or L—We do not fight with others. L—We do not hurt dogs or cats. L—We go to school every day. R—We keep our hands and feet to ourselves. R—We clean up our toys.

Week 15—Geography

Day 1
1. c
2. b
3. Responses will vary.

Day 2
1. d
2. Responses will vary.

Day 3
1. c
2. Responses will be added to map.
3. Responses will vary.

Day 4
1. c
2. d
3. Responses will vary.

Day 5
Responses will be added to map.

Week 16—Economics

Day 1
1. a
2. c
3. d

Day 2
1. b
2. d
3. c

Day 3
1. d
2. Responses will vary but may include: desks; chairs; whiteboard; paper; pencils, and so on.
3. Responses will vary but may include: custodian; secretary; education/teaching assistant, and so on. The government pays for their services.

Day 4
1. c
2. Responses will be added to graphic.
3. Responses will vary but may include: police; firefighters; mayor; and so on.

Day 5
police officer: S construction worker: S
firefighter: S park cleaner: S road: G street
sign: G mayor: S librarian: S traffic light: G

Week 17—History

Day 1
1. d
2. b, d (allow for a)
3. c

© Shell Education

ANSWER KEY *(cont.)*

Day 2
1. a
2. d
3. Responses will vary.

Day 3
1. b
2. d
3. Responses will vary but may state a preference for building in modern times as the process is easier and faster.

Day 4
1. c
2. Responses will vary but may include similarities such as: students; teacher; desks; learning; and so on.
3. Responses will vary but may state a preference for modern times as there are many more benefits for students including, for example, technology.

Day 5
Responses will vary but may refer to the following: cooking over a fire; milking a cow; writing on slates; having children of varying ages within one classroom; students cleaning the classroom; parent roles; home cooking; candle light; and sleeping in a loft.

Week 18—Civics

Day 1
1. d
2. b
3. d

Day 2
1. b
2. c
3. d

Day 3
1. d
2. b
3. Responses will vary but may relate to the vice president helping the president or standing in for him or her.

Day 4
1. b
2. Responses will vary.

Day 5
Same: They serve for four or eight years; work in the White House; are part of the executive branch; and work for the country. Different: The president is the leader of the country, the executive branch, and the military; has more power; signs laws; can veto laws; chooses people to work for the cabinet; and lives in the White House. The vice president helps the president; can stand in for the president; and can break a tie in the Senate.

Week 19—Geography

Day 1
1. d
2. c

Day 2
1. a, b, d
2. d
3. Responses will vary.

Day 3
1. c
2. Responses will vary but may refer to water transportation or water for drinking, washing, and watering crops.

Day 4
1. d
2. c

Day 5
Responses will vary but may relate to the following:
mountains: ski; rock climb
north: make a snow person; wear warm clothes
rural area: have a farm; see forests or open land
rain: play indoors; read

© Shell Education

ANSWER KEY *(cont.)*

Week 20—Economics

Day 1
1. d
2. c
3. a, c, d

Day 2
1. c
2. d
3. b

Day 3
1. a, b, d
2. paper towels; dish soap; tissues
3. Responses will vary but may include: ask parents to supply what is needed; buy some of the items; or ask the principal if there are any in the school.

Day 4
1. c
2. Responses will vary but may include sharing or trading.
3. Responses will vary but may include sharing or asking family members if there are more cookies.

Day 5
Correct ideas:
1. Do not water the lawns.
2. Do not take a long shower.
3. Use a rain barrel to collect the little bit of rain water.
4. Use recycled water for the yard.
5. Do not wash your car so often.
6. Plant gardens that do not need as much water.

Week 21—History

Day 1
1. d
2. a
3. c

Day 2
1. d
2. b
3. b

Day 3
1. a
2. two of the following: baseball, football, running/track and field
3. Responses may include: he was American Indian; he won two gold medals; he won medals for his country.

Day 4
1. c
2. The English kept Pocahontas prisoner for a long time. John Rolfe married her.
3. Responses will vary.

Day 5
1. Responses will vary.

Week 22—Civics

Day 1
1. b
2. c
3. d

Day 2
1. c
2. b
3. c

Day 3
1. d
2. Responses will vary but may include: street repairs; library; garbage collection; recreation center; and so on.

© Shell Education

ANSWER KEY *(cont.)*

Day 4
1. c
2. c
3. Responses will vary.

Day 5
federal government: writes laws such as those for banks; prints money; can send the military to help people; includes the Supreme Court
local government: some services are public libraries; parks; transportation; police.
same: protect people; offer services to help people
different: offer different services (military/police, war, money, laws with other countries)

Week 23—Geography

Day 1
1. c
2. b

Day 2
1. c
2. b
3. Responses will vary but may relate to flooding.

Day 3
1. d
2. c
3. Responses will vary but may relate to it being easier to move horses and/or machinery across flat land.

Day 4
1. a
2. c
3. Responses will vary.

Day 5
1. circle: flat land; river/water
X: earthquake, tornado, hurricane
2. Responses will vary.

Week 24—Economics

Day 1
1. c
2. c
3. d

Day 2
1. c
2. d
3. b

Day 3
1. b
2. 1 and 3 are not working. They are playing.
3. 2 and 4 are harder chores and may pay more.

Day 4
1. c
2. Responses will vary.

Day 5
Responses will vary.

Week 25—History

Day 1
1. d
2. b
3. a

Day 2
1. d
2. b
3. Responses will vary but may relate to: traveling quickly; sending letters and packages quickly; or use by the military.

Day 3
1. d
2. Responses will vary but may relate to size, positioning of wheels, pedals, and so on.
3. Responses will vary.

© Shell Education

ANSWER KEY *(cont.)*

Day 4
1. 4, 3, 1, 2
2. Responses will vary.

Day 5
Responses will vary.

Week 26—Civics

Day 1
1. c
2. d
3. b

Day 2
1. b
2. c
3. c

Day 3
1. c
2. c
3. to treat everyone well, regardless of a person's age, culture, gender, or religion

Day 4
1. b
2. Responses will vary but should provide examples of telling the truth.
3. Responses will vary but may relate to cooperation, helping, caring, sharing, and so on.

Day 5
pursuit of happiness—Pursue happiness but respect the rights of others.
truth—People do not lie.
patriotism—Love your country.
common good—Work with other people to help everyone.
equality—Treat all people in the same way.
liberty—You are free to speak and write what you think.
democracy—The leader with the most votes wins.

Week 27—Geography

Day 1
1. c
2. c

Day 2
1. d
2. a
3. Responses will vary.

Day 3
1. c
2. d
3. Responses will vary.

Day 4
1. c
2. b
3. Responses will vary but may include: do not pollute; clean up; recycle; reuse.

Day 5
1. Responses will vary but may relate to:
    same: parks and tree planting
    different: buildings; bridges; roads
2. Drawings will vary.

Week 28—Economics

Day 1
1. a, b, c
2. b
3. c

Day 2
1. c
2. b

Day 3
1. d
2. Cilla made lemonade that cost more. Dee and Lars made a stand that cost more.
3. Cilla's lemonade will probably sell best as it is made with fresh ingredients. She will get the best benefit.

203

ANSWER KEY *(cont.)*

Day 4
1. b
2. Responses will vary but may relate to: spending less on their display; displaying in an attractive way; letting customers try the toys; and so on.
3. Responses will vary but may relate to: making signs; displaying in an attractive manner; and selling items that are in good shape.

Day 5
Circle good choices: Work from home. Use some gold that is mixed with silver ($5). Buy a used spinning wheel; it works well. Wear his old clothes to work. Use his own van. Weave the yarn. Make nice scarves to sell. Responses will vary but may include keeping costs low and selling scarves.

Week 29—History

Day 1
1. c
2. Today: Use a remote control. Long ago: walk to the TV and press or turn the button.
3. TV from today will offer better picture and sound quality, and more viewing choices.

Day 2
1. d
2. c
3. b

Day 3
1. d
2. b

3. Responses will vary but may relate to: word processing; recording; drawing; playing games; and so on.

Day 4
1. c
2. People use cameras to help remember their families, friends, and events. Today, people use cameras for many reasons: to remember; to share; to communicate on social media; and so on.

Day 5
Responses will vary. The following are possible responses:
television: remote control; color; more channels
telephone: wireless; screens
computer: smaller; more functions
camera: no film; smaller

Week 30—Civics

Day 1
1. c
2. d
3. d

Day 2
1. c
2. d
3. They pay more taxes.

Day 3
1. d
2. Responses will vary but may include: police officers; firefighters; teachers; and so on.

Day 4
1. b
2. Responses will vary.

ANSWER KEY (cont.)

Day 5

Paid for by taxes: the president; public school; city bus; garbage collectors; city workers; public library, public library books; mayor; city hall; judge; workers fixing holes in the street; fire truck; police station; teachers

Week 31—Geography

Day 1
1. c
2. b
3. d

Day 2
1. d
2. b
3. Responses will vary but may relate to mine cave in or collapse.

Day 3
1. a
2. Responses will vary but may relate to: many people like eating different fish; not depleting one kind of fish; allows for more fishing jobs, and so on.

Day 4
1. b
2. Responses will vary but students may respond that they wear wool clothing when it is cold and cotton or linen clothing when it is warm.

Day 5

Responses will vary but may relate to:
oil and gas: to run our cars and heat buildings; to make plastics, clothing, and paint
mines: diamonds; copper; gold; silver; sand and gravel
fishing: fish; seafood
fiber: sweaters; hats; mittens

Week 32—Economics

Day 1
1. c
2. d
3. b

Day 2
1. c
2. a

Day 3
1. X on computer; remote-controlled helicopter; toy train; soccer ball
2. Responses will vary.
3. d

Day 4
1. Response added to chart; total $35
2. c
3. once per month

Day 5

bank; account; passbook; interest; long; ATM; card; password

Week 33—History

Day 1
1. b
2. c
3. b, c, d

Day 2
1. d
2. Responses will vary but may relate to: use of metal and plastic; garages; apartment buildings.

Day 3
1. d
2. Responses may include: bus; car; subway train; taxi; cycling; walking.
3. Responses will vary.

Day 4
1. d
2. b
3. Responses will vary.

© Shell Education

ANSWER KEY *(cont.)*

Day 5
Responses will vary.

Week 34—Civics

Day 1
1. c
2. d
3. a

Day 2
1. d
2. c
3. Responses will vary but may relate to Earhart standing for equal rights for men and women and showing courage.

Day 3
1. b
2. d
3. Responses will vary but all of these worked to help other people.

Day 4
1. d
2. Responses will vary but may relate to Code Talkers keeping soldiers safe.
3. Responses will vary.

Day 5
1. Helen Keller, Theodore Roosevelt, Sojourner Truth, George Washington, Martin Luther King Jr., and Amelia Earhart
2. Responses will vary but may relate to courage, helping others, and showing leadership.

Week 35—Geography

Day 1
1. d (allow for a)
2. b
3. a, b, c (allow for d)

Day 2
1. c
2. b
3. fruits from Mexico; nuts from Brazil; meat from Canada; responses will vary as to kinds of food from other countries

Day 3
1. c
2. Responses will vary.

Day 4
1. d
2. d
3. Responses will vary but will relate to different forms of transportation.

Day 5
People move by bus, car, taxi, train, boat, airplane, and on foot; to avoid war, to find work, to find better weather, to go to school
Ideas move by mail, phone, email, text, television, newspaper, Internet, computers; to communicate, inform, buy
Things move by pipeline, truck, boat, train, airplane; so people can buy them

ANSWER KEY *(cont.)*

Week 36—Economics

Day 1
1. d
2. c
3. a

Day 2
1. c
2. d
3. cows and/or milk; dairy farms

Day 3
1. b
2.
   1. The wheat grows in the field.
   2. The farmer harvests the wheat.
   3. The wheat travels to a factory.
   4. The wheat is milled. It becomes flour.
   5. The flour is put in bags.
   6. The flour travels to a bakery.
   7. The baker makes the bread.
   8. The baker sells the bread.
   9. We buy and eat the bread.

Day 4
1. c
2. Responses will vary.
3. Responses will vary but may relate to seeing cotton plants and machinery.

Day 5
1. tomatoes in the field
2. tomato harvest
3. transport to factory
4. factory: wash, crush, and make sauce
5. transport to store
6. sauce on the store shelves

Response Rubric

Teacher Directions: The answer key provides answers for the multiple-choice and short-answer questions. This rubric can be used for any open-ended questions where student responses vary. Evaluate student work to determine how many points out of 12 students earn.

Student Name: _____

	4 Points	3 Points	2 Points	1 Point
Content Knowledge	Gives right answers. Answers are based on text and prior knowledge.	Gives right answers based on text.	Gives mostly right answers based on text.	Gives incorrect answers.
Analysis	Thinks about the content, and draws strong inferences/conclusions.	Thinks about the content, and draws mostly correct inferences/conclusions.	Thinks about the content, and draws somewhat correct inferences/conclusions.	Thinks about the content, and draws incorrect inferences/conclusions.
Explanation	Explains and supports answers fully.	Explains and supports answers with some evidence.	Explains and supports answers with little evidence.	Provides no support for answers.

Total: _____

© Shell Education

Practice Page Item Analysis

Teacher Directions: Record how many multiple-choice questions students answered correctly. Then, record their rubric totals for Day 5. Total the four weeks of scores, and record that number in the Overall column.

Circle Week Range: 1–4 5–8 9–12 13–16 17–20 21–24 25–28 29–32 33–36						
Student Name	**Day 1** Text Analysis	**Day 2** Text Analysis	**Day 3** Primary Source or Visual Text	**Day 4** Making Connections	**Day 5** Synthesis and Application	**Overall**
Ryan	2, 3, 3, 3	3, 3, 3, 3	3, 3, 3, 3	3, 3, 2, 3	9, 10, 10, 12	87

Student Item Analysis By Discipline

Teacher Directions: Record how many multiple-choice questions students answered correctly. Then, record their rubric totals for Day 5. Total the four weeks of scores, and record that number in the Overall column.

Student Name:

History Weeks	Day 1 Text Analysis	Day 2 Text Analysis	Day 3 Primary Source or Visual Text	Day 4 Making Connections	Day 5 Synthesis and Application	Overall
1						
5						
9						
13						
17						
21						
25						
29						
33						

Civics Weeks	Day 1 Text Analysis	Day 2 Text Analysis	Day 3 Primary Source or Visual Text	Day 4 Making Connections	Day 5 Synthesis and Application	Overall
2						
6						
10						
14						
18						
22						
26						
30						
34						

© *Shell Education*

Student Item Analysis By Discipline *(cont.)*

Student Name:

Geography Weeks	Day 1 Text Analysis	Day 2 Text Analysis	Day 3 Primary Source or Visual Text	Day 4 Making Connections	Day 5 Synthesis and Application	Overall
3						
7						
11						
15						
19						
23						
27						
31						
35						

Economics Weeks	Day 1 Text Analysis	Day 2 Text Analysis	Day 3 Primary Source or Visual Text	Day 4 Making Connections	Day 5 Synthesis and Application	Overall
4						
8						
12						
16						
20						
24						
28						
32						
36						

© Shell Education

NORTH AMERICA

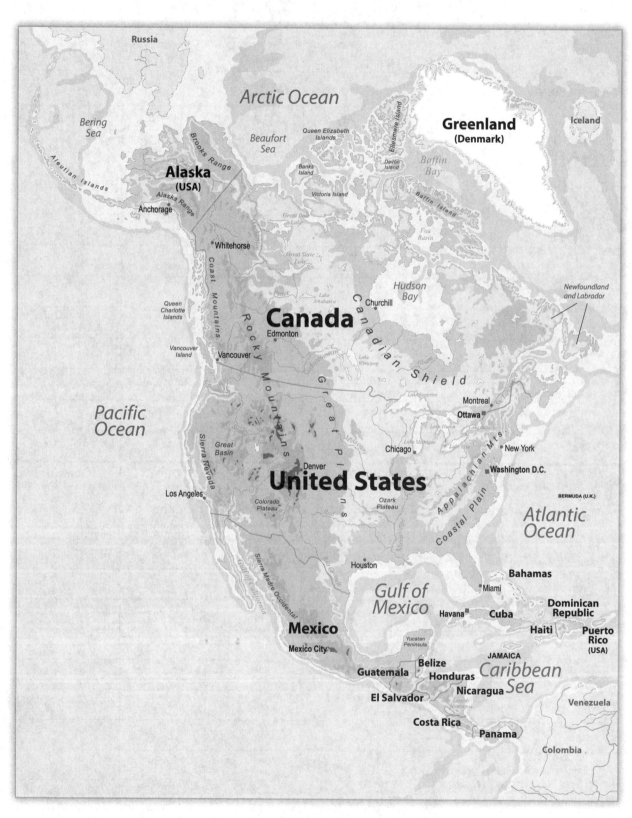

Russia

Arctic Ocean

Bering
Sea

Beaufort
Sea

Queen Elizabeth
Islands

Ellesmere Island

Greenland
(Denmark)

Iceland

Aleutian Islands

Brooks Range

Alaska
(USA)

Alaska Range

Anchorage

Banks
Island

*Devon
Island*

Victoria Island

*Baffin
Bay*

Baffin Island

*Great Bear
Lake*

*Fox
Basin*

Whitehorse

*Great Slave
Lake*

Coast Mountains

*Queen
Charlotte
Islands*

Peace

*Lake
Athabasca*

Churchill

Canada

Hudson
Bay

*Newfoundland
and Labrador*

Rocky Mountains

Edmonton

Canadian Shield

*Vancouver
Island*

Vancouver

Saskatchewan

*Lake
Winnipeg*

Albany

**Pacific
Ocean**

Great Plains

Lake Superior

St. Lawrence

Montreal

Ottawa

Lake Huron

Lake Ontario

New York

Chicago

Lake Michigan

Missouri

Washington D.C.

Sierra Nevada

*Great
Basin*

Denver

United States

Appalachian Mts.

Los Angeles

*Colorado
Plateau*

Ozark
Plateau

Coastal Plain

BERMUDA (U.K.)

**Atlantic
Ocean**

Rio Grande

Houston

Bahamas

Miami

Sierra Madre Occidental

*Gulf of
California*

*Gulf of
Mexico*

Havana

Cuba

**Dominican
Republic**

Haiti

**Puerto
Rico**
(USA)

Mexico

*Yucatan
Peninsula*

JAMAICA

*Caribbean
Sea*

Mexico City

Guatemala

Belize

Honduras

El Salvador

Nicaragua

Venezuela

Costa Rica

Panama

Colombia

POLITICAL MAP OF THE UNITED STATES

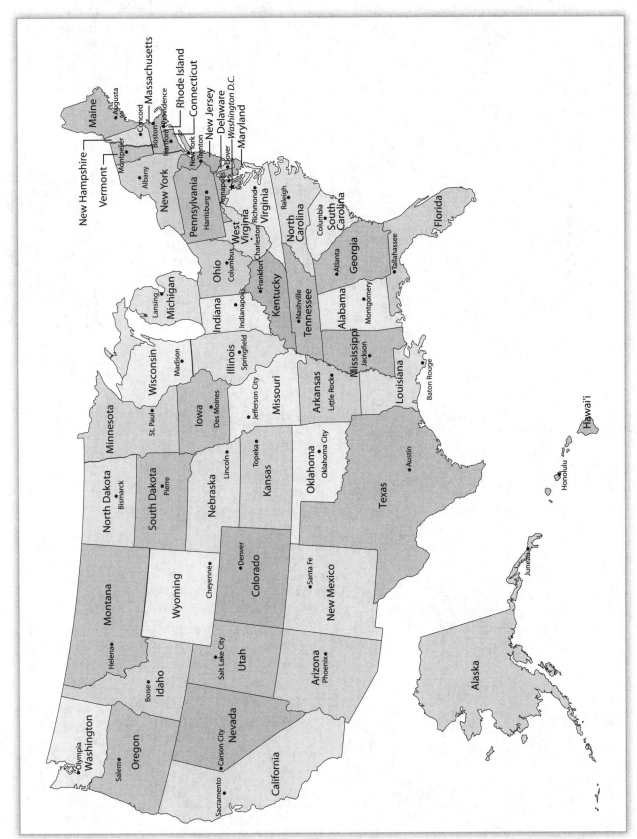

© Shell Education

51394—180 Days of Social Studies

PHYSICAL MAP OF THE UNITED STATES

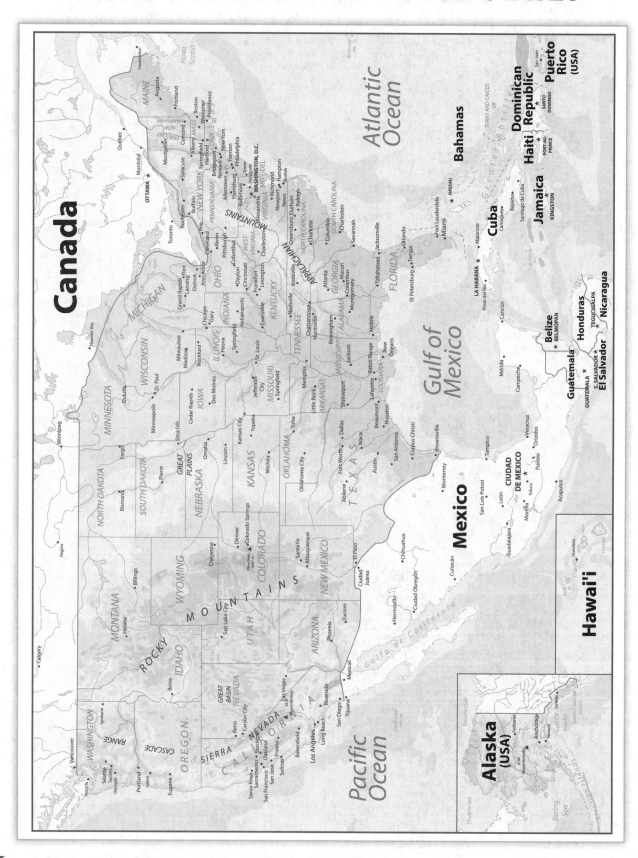

Digital Resources

To access the digital resources, go to this website and enter the following code: 41540171. www.teachercreatedmaterials.com/administrators/download-files/.

Rubric and Analysis Sheets

Resource	Filename
Response Rubric	responserubric.pdf
Practice Page Item Analysis	itemanalysis.pdf
	itemanalysis.docx
	itemanalysis.xlsx
Student Item Analysis by Discipline	socialstudiesanalysis.pdf
	socialstudiesanalysis.docx
	socialstudiesanalysis.xlsx

Standards and Themes

Resource	Filename
Weekly Topics and Themes	topicsthemes.pdf
Standards Charts	standards.pdf

© Shell Education

NOTES

© Shell Education